Stackable Credential Pipelines and Equity for Low-Income Individuals

Evidence from Colorado and Ohio

LINDSAY DAUGHERTY (RAND CORPORATION)
PETER RILEY BAHR (UNIVERSITY OF MICHIGAN)
PETER NGUYEN (RAND CORPORATION)
JENNIFER MAY-TRIFILETTI (UNIVERSITY OF MICHIGAN)
ROONEY COLUMBUS (UNIVERSITY OF MICHIGAN)
JONAH KUSHNER (RAND CORPORATION)

Sponsored by the Ascendium Education Group

For more information on this publication, visit **www.rand.org/t/RRA2484-1**.

About RAND

The RAND Corporation is a research organization that develops solutions to public policy challenges to help make communities throughout the world safer and more secure, healthier and more prosperous. RAND is nonprofit, nonpartisan, and committed to the public interest. To learn more about RAND, visit www.rand.org.

Research Integrity

Our mission to help improve policy and decisionmaking through research and analysis is enabled through our core values of quality and objectivity and our unwavering commitment to the highest level of integrity and ethical behavior. To help ensure our research and analysis are rigorous, objective, and nonpartisan, we subject our research publications to a robust and exacting quality-assurance process; avoid both the appearance and reality of financial and other conflicts of interest through staff training, project screening, and a policy of mandatory disclosure; and pursue transparency in our research engagements through our commitment to the open publication of our research findings and recommendations, disclosure of the source of funding of published research, and policies to ensure intellectual independence. For more information, visit www.rand.org/about/research-integrity.

RAND's publications do not necessarily reflect the opinions of its research clients and sponsors.

About This Report

Beginning in the mid-2000s, federal, state, and local initiatives have encouraged education and training providers to build *stackable credentials*, a series of postsecondary credentials that can be earned over time and that build on each other to prepare individuals with the evolving knowledge and skills needed throughout a career. By offering flexible pathways that allow individuals to earn credentials incrementally and work as they earn credentials, stackable credentials might increase economic and educational opportunity for low-income individuals and other communities who have not been well served in traditional degree programs (e.g., low-income individuals, older learners). However, there is limited evidence on the effectiveness of stackable credential pipelines in achieving these aims. In this report, we focus on Colorado and Ohio, two states pursuing stackable credential initiatives. We took a mixed methods approach to investigating stackable credential pipelines. We examined patterns in credential-stacking for low-income students relative to middle- and high-income students and explored four systemic barriers that might limit opportunities for low-income individuals to stack credentials.

RAND Education and Labor and University of Michigan

This study was undertaken by RAND Education and Labor in collaboration with the Center for the Study of Higher and Postsecondary Education at the University of Michigan–Ann Arbor. RAND Education and Labor is a division of the RAND Corporation that conducts research on early childhood through postsecondary education programs, workforce development, and programs and policies affecting workers, entrepreneurship, and financial literacy and decisionmaking. The University of Michigan-Ann Arbor is the flagship research university of the state of Michigan, serving the people of the state and the world through preeminence in creating, communicating, preserving, and applying knowledge, art, and academic values and in developing leaders and citizens who will challenge the present and enrich the future.

This study was sponsored by Ascendium Education Group, a foundation that focuses on giving learners from low-income backgrounds more opportunities to succeed by fostering systemic change in postsecondary education and training. The opinions expressed are those of the authors and do not represent the views of Ascendium Education Group.

More information about RAND can be found at www.rand.org. Questions about this report should be directed to Lindsay Daugherty at ldaugher@rand.org, and questions about RAND Education and Labor should be directed to educationandlabor@rand.org.

Acknowledgments

This study would not have been possible without close collaboration with our partners at the Colorado Community College System, including Landon Pirius and Stacie Amaya, and our partners at the Ohio Department of Higher Education, including Tom Sudkamp, Cheri Rice, Paula Compton, Patty Klein, and Sherry Chadwell. We also benefited from regular input from advisory committees and thank the members of these committees for their time and valuable perspectives. In Colorado, the advisory group included Vicki Aycock, Tony Bowling, Julie Brower, Meghan Davis, Eric Dunker, Noah Geisel, Janel Highfill, Caitlin McKennie, Melissa Martin, Kim Poast, Chris Rasmussen, Daniel Sandoval, Will Simpkins, Linda Van Doren, Michael Vente, Seth Ward, and Ayelet Zur-Nayberg. We thank Ruthanne Orihuela for her input on the report. In Ohio, the advisory group included George Bilonkonsky, Bill Bussey, Amy Dunbaugh, Michael Evans, Todd

Foley, Lada Gibson-Shreve, Lauren Massie, Tracey Meilander, Daniel Rizo-Patron, Tom Prendergast, Mike Suver, Jarrod Tudor, and Rick Woodfield.

Our data providers were essential to supporting this work. The Ohio Longitudinal Data Archive is a project of the Ohio Education Research Center (http://www.oerc.osu.edu/) and provides researchers with centralized access to administrative data. The OLDA is managed by The Ohio State University's CHRR (https://chrr.osu.edu/) in collaboration with Ohio's state workforce and education agencies (http://www.ohioanalytics.gov/), with those agencies providing oversight and funding. For information on OLDA sponsors, see http://chrr.osu.edu/projects/ohio-longitudinal-data-archive. In Colorado, data were provided by the Colorado Community College System. We thank Samantha Kalinowski and Sean Flohr for their assistance pulling together data.

We appreciate the helpful reviews from Michelle Van Noy (Rutgers University) and Jenna Kramer (RAND) and believe that these reviews greatly strengthened the report. We also received valuable input on the study's framework at the outset of the project from Michelle and three other expert advisors working on related issues, Brett Visger (Education Strategy Group), Iris Palmer (New America), and Nan Travers (Intrascope).

Finally, we are grateful to our funder, Ascendium Education Group, for its support of this research and thoughtful perspectives on the work. We thank Carolynn Lee and Maryann Rainey for their guidance and feedback.

Summary

The Issue: Stackable Credentials and Equity

According to the U.S. Department of Labor, *stackable credentials* are defined as a "sequence of credentials that can be accumulated over time to build up an individual's qualifications and help that individual move along a career pathway to further education and different responsibilities, and potentially higher-paying jobs" (Employment and Training Administration, 2010, p. 6). These more-structured education and training pathways in applied fields, such as health care, information technology (IT), and manufacturing, can offer individuals the opportunity to earn short-term credentials that provide early job possibilities and to continue to earn credentials over time to expand career options in their fields. Studies indicate that a substantial proportion of students stack credentials (Bailey and Belfield, 2017a; Bohn and McConville, 2018; Daugherty et. al, 2020), and stacking credentials can lead to increased earnings (Bohn, Jackson, and McConville, 2019; Daugherty and Anderson, 2021; Meyer, Bird, and Castleman, 2020).

One of the reasons that many states and institutions have begun to adopt stackable credential initiatives is the hope that they will offer additional on-ramps into postsecondary education and more-flexible credentialing opportunities that could be particularly attractive to individuals who have been underserved by traditional degree programs, including low-income individuals, older individuals, and individuals of color (Austin et al., 2012; Center for Occupational Research and Development, 2018; Wilson, 2016). However, there is relatively little evidence on whether stackable credentials improve education and economic outcomes for these groups. Studies indicate wide variation in the labor market returns from stacking different credentials, suggesting that only some of these credentials offer value to individuals and raising concerns that many individuals could end up earning credentials that do not provide meaningful economic opportunities (Bohn, Jackson, and McConville, 2019; Daugherty and Anderson, 2021; Meyer, Bird, and Castleman, 2020). Several studies have examined subgroup differences in rates of stacking and labor market returns and found that adult learners and students of color might be less likely to benefit from stacking credentials (Bohn, Jackson and McConville, 2019; Bohn and McConville, 2018; Daugherty and Anderson, 2021; Daugherty et al., 2020; Giani and Fox, 2016; Meyer, Bird, and Castleman, 2020). However, little is known about rates of stacking and differences in the returns from stacking between middle- and high-income individuals, as a group, and low-income individuals.

In addition, little work has been done to explore what factors might be driving inequities within stackable credential pipelines. There are various potential barriers that low-income individuals and other historically underserved populations might face, and some of these barriers might be related to the way in which credentials are offered within postsecondary systems and the degree to which students are aware of the stackable credential opportunities available to them. We focused on four potential barriers in stackable credential pipelines:

- *Limited opportunities to stack credentials in some fields:* Rates of stacking vary widely across fields. If low-income individuals tend to pursue education and careers in fields that have been slower to scale stackable credential programs, these individuals might have limited opportunities to benefit from stacking credentials.
- *Limited opportunities to stack credentials in some institutions:* Students (especially low-income students) are often constrained to pursuing education at their local institutions, and the stackable programs offered by their institutions are therefore critical to shaping opportunities to stack. If stackable credential programs vary widely across institutions and institutions that disproportionately serve low-income

individuals offer fewer stackable credential programs, low-income individuals will have limited opportunities to benefit from stacking credentials.

- *Insufficient information and resources to identify and stack credentials of value:* Stackable credentials can be challenging for individuals to understand and navigate. Individuals need clear information on how programs stack and the value each credential offers in terms of employment opportunities. If informational resources are insufficient and low-income individuals face particular barriers to accessing information on high-value stackable credential programs, low-income individuals might be less likely to pursue these credentials.

- *Challenges moving from noncredit to credit programs:* Stackable credential pipelines should allow individuals to move between noncredit and programs that are offered for college credit. Low-income individuals are more likely to start in noncredit programs, and, if these individuals face challenges moving from noncredit to credit programs, lower rates of stacking might be observed.

Building better evidence on credential-stacking and how it might differ for low-income and middle- and high-income individuals can help states and institutions determine whether and how to continue scaling these programs. Describing potential barriers to equity identify where stackable credential pipelines can be strengthened to ensure that they advance education and employment opportunities for low-income communities.

Our Approach to Building Evidence on Stackable Credentials and Equity

Our study focused on Colorado and Ohio, two states which are deeply engaged in efforts to build stackable credential pipelines at the state, system, and institutional levels. We drew on mixed methods analysis to build evidence on stackable credentials and equity. First, we leveraged statewide administrative data to identify low-income and middle- and high-income certificate-earners and examine the types of credentials these certificate-earners went on to stack and the earnings gains experienced over time. Second, we conducted interviews with institutional administrators who oversee stackable programs and state and system leaders to learn about the factors that might contribute to the four systemic barriers and possible approaches to overcoming those barriers.

There are several limitations to our approach. We could not determine from our data which credentials were designed to be stackable, so, while we observe individuals who happened to earn multiple credentials, we are not able to determine which credentials and programs were designed with that intent. Our sample focused on individuals who earned initial credit-bearing certificates at community colleges and Ohio Technical Centers (OTCs). We also lacked data on noncredit credentials (e.g., certificates, certifications) offered outside OTCs. As a result, we focused on a subset of all of the individuals earning certificates, and we did not observe some of the credentials that individuals earned. In addition, we were missing income data for nearly one-quarter of Ohio students and nearly one-fifth of Colorado students. The qualitative analysis focused on a subset of institutions and stakeholders, and the perspectives we gathered on the four barriers were limited to those held by a subset of administrators, faculty, and system leaders (i.e., we did not have student perspectives). Despite these limitations, we believe that our analyses capture a major portion of the credential-stacking taking place in these two states, and our findings provide valuable insights into how major components of the stackable credential ecosystem are contributing to equity.

Key Findings on Stackable Credentials and Equity

Given limited evidence on the degree to which low-income individuals are stacking credentials and concerns that stackable credentials might not be providing value to all groups, we examined administrative data to compare patterns of stacking and returns from stacking for low-income individuals with those of middle- and high-income individuals. We found that low-income certificate-earners tended to earn multiple credentials (i.e., stacked credentials) and went on to earn longer-term credentials (i.e., stacked vertically) at higher rates than middle- and high-income certificate-earners. Low-income vertical stackers experienced positive economic returns from stacking, narrowing the earnings gap between low-income individuals and middle- and high-income individuals. These findings suggest that stackable credentials might help advance equity for low-income individuals overall. The positive findings for credential-stacking among low-income individuals stand in contrast to findings for other historically underserved populations, such as older learners and individuals of color, which show some evidence indicating lower rates of stacking and lower returns from stacking relative to younger individuals and White individuals. (Bohn, Jackson, and McConville, 2019; Daugherty and Anderson, 2021)

We then examined mixed methods evidence on our four systemic barriers. The findings are summarized in Table S.1. We found that, while low-income individuals were benefiting from stacking, rates of stacking and returns to earnings varied by field. For example, nursing and allied health generally had low rates of stacking but high returns for those who did stack, while education and family and consumer sciences (FCS) had high rates of stacking but more-limited returns. All three of these fields had relatively high concentrations of low-income certificate-earners. IT and manufacturing and engineering technology (MET) had both high rates of stacking and high returns from stacking, but low-income individuals earned certificates in these fields at lower rates. We cannot pinpoint the specific factors driving student sorting into different fields; that is a topic for future research. However, to the degree that these patterns reflect systematic differences in the availability of stackable programs to low-income individuals and awareness of the opportunities, there might be ways that states and institutions can strengthen stackable credential pipelines to ensure that low-income individuals are benefiting. As outlined in Table S.1, institutional staff and state and system leaders in Colorado and Ohio identified several factors that might be hindering the development of stackable credential programs in certain fields and institutions, as well as factors that might be limiting the information individuals have on stackable programs and credential value. Stakeholders also provided valuable suggestions on actions that states and institutions could take to strengthen these aspects of stackable credential pipelines.

We found wide variation in stackable programs across institutions, with rates of stacking ranging from 22 percent to 50 percent in Colorado and 20 percent to 63 percent in Ohio. However, we did not find that institutions with low rates of stacking served larger percentages of low-income students, so variation in opportunities to stack across institutions might not be a major barrier to equity for this group. Nonetheless, wide variation in opportunities to stack across institutions might be concerning, because individuals often are tied to their local institutions by work or family obligations, meaning that some individuals would be constrained to these low-stacking opportunity institutions. As outlined in Table S.1, stakeholders identified factors that might be limiting opportunities to stack across institutions and opportunities to support stackable programs in institutions that offer fewer options.

And finally, while we had limited data on noncredit credentials, the data available from Ohio suggest that individuals who earn noncredit certificates are commonly low-income, and these individuals who earn noncredit certificates rarely go on to earn credit-bearing credentials. Stakeholders identified several major factors contributing to this, as shown in Table S.1. Both Colorado and Ohio are pursuing noncredit-to-credit articulation frameworks and other initiatives that will help address this barrier, and stakeholders suggested several other efforts that might improve noncredit-to-credit transitions.

TABLE S.1

Evidence on the Four Systemic Barriers to Stacking

Potential Systemic Barrier	Evidence on Inequities from Administrative Data	Stakeholder Perceptions of Factors Driving Barrier	Stakeholder Perceptions of Solutions to Barrier
Limited opportunities to stack credentials in some fields	• Low-income certificate-earners were concentrated in some fields with lower stacking rates (e.g., education and FCS) but also in some fields with higher stacking rates (e.g., mechanics). • Low-income certificate-earners were underrepresented in some fields with the highest stacking rates (e.g., IT, MET).	• Limited workforce needs and limited industry engagement • Substantial program startup costs • Administrative burden • Challenges with faculty recruitment • Insufficient access to equipment and instructional resources • Competition between institutions	• Improve coordination with industry • Provide financial assistance to support startup costs • Improve administrative processes for program improvement • Strengthen institutional capacity to recruit faculty • Improve coordination across institutions • Provide additional funding for instructional resources
Limited opportunities to stack credentials in some institutions	• Stacking rates varied substantially across institutions within a state. • There was no evidence of a systematic relationship between an institution's concentration of low-income certificate-earners and its stacking rate.	• Same as above	• Same as above
Insufficient information and resources to identify and stack credentials of value	• Low-income certificate-earners were concentrated in some fields with low returns (e.g., education and FCS) and some fields with higher returns (e.g., nursing, mechanics). • Low-income certificate-earners were underrepresented in some fields with the highest returns (e.g., IT, MET).	• Common perceptions of college credentials and certain fields • Limited messaging from employers about credential value • Constraints on faculty and advisors	• Enhance informational resources on stackable credentials and credential value • Better leverage career services • Provide institutions with additional resources to enhance advising support • Encourage greater partnership with industry
Challenges moving from noncredit to credit programs	• Low-income and middle- and high-income noncredit certificate-earners stacked at higher rates than credit certificate-earners. • Both low-income and middle- and high-income noncredit certificate-earners who stacked almost always earned a second noncredit credential and rarely completed credit certificates or degrees.	• Administrative burden • Lack of alignment between noncredit learning and credit coursework • Variation in standards and perceptions of quality • Limited awareness of articulation opportunities	• Streamline administrative processes • Align noncredit learning experiences and credit courses • Strengthen coordination between noncredit and credit departments and institutions • Invest in outreach to improve awareness

Takeaways for States, Systems, and Institutions

Our findings from Colorado and Ohio suggest some broader lessons for policymakers and practitioners about scaling stackable credentials and ensuring that these pipelines are equitable.

Continue to scale initiatives that help individuals stack credentials and ensure that these credentials advance equity for historically underserved populations. Our evidence suggests that stacking credentials advances equity for low-income individuals. Low-income certificate-earners stack credentials—and stack vertically—at higher rates, and gaps in earnings shrink as credentials stack. However, this stands in contrast to some of the evidence for other historically underserved groups (e.g., individuals of color, older learners), suggesting that we still need to understand more about how different communities are accessing credentials and why some individuals are less likely to stack credentials or experience labor market benefits.

Identify and scale credentials of value. Ensuring equitable stackable credential pipelines means making sure that individuals have access to credentials that offer meaningful job opportunities and growth in earnings (i.e., credentials of value). We identified fields, such as IT, MET, mechanics, and nursing, that offer high returns to individuals. States and institutions should focus efforts on scaling programs that offer value and discouraging the development of low-value programs.

Invest resources strategically to ensure that stackable credential pipelines are equitable and identify opportunities for coordination and alignment. Many of the recommendations from stakeholders for addressing gaps in stackable credential pipelines focused on devoting additional resources to cover program startup costs, equipment, faculty, and other inputs that make the development of new programs in some fields and institutions difficult. The need for greater cooperation and alignment was another important theme. These are two areas in which state agencies and systems can play a valuable role in supporting stackable credential efforts.

Ensure that low-income individuals and other historically underserved populations have clear information on stackable programs and the economic value of credentials. While we were not able to directly examine the use of information for decisionmaking or talk directly with individuals, the stakeholders we spoke with expressed concerns about the information available on stackable credentials. When we reviewed websites, we found the quality and content of information was widely variable. Stackable credentials can only help advance equity if low-income individuals and other historically underserved populations are aware of the opportunities and able to identify the credentials that will provide meaningful career opportunities.

Continue to pursue efforts to support noncredit-to-credit movement, including the collection of better noncredit data. Institutions and states have made greater efforts to bridge noncredit and credit credentials through articulation agreements, shared program development, and advising initiatives. These efforts should begin to show in the data, and states and institutions should continue to expand these efforts. We had limited data to examine noncredit credentials and noncredit-to-credit movement; states should collect better administrative data on noncredit programs to track stacking and more systematically assess program value.

Conclusion

The evidence in this report suggests that stacking credentials might help advance equity, with promising patterns in credential-stacking and earnings for low-income individuals. However, there continue to be areas in which low-income individuals and other historically underserved groups face challenges stacking credentials that lead to improved economic outcomes. States and institutions should continue to support stackable credential initiatives and scale credentials of value, but they should also continue to look critically at how these programs are structured and how individuals are moving through them to ensure that stackable credential pipelines are accessible and support equitable experiences and outcomes.

Contents

Figures and Tables

Figures

Tables

CHAPTER 1

Introduction

States and institutions across the United States are pursuing initiatives that support the design of *stackable credentials*, defined by the U.S. Department of Labor as a "sequence of credentials that can be accumulated over time to build up an individual's qualifications and help that individual move along a career pathway to further education and different responsibilities, and potentially higher-paying jobs" (Employment and Training Administration, 2010, p. 6). Stackable credentials typically encourage individuals to start their education with certificates, short-term credentials that require anywhere from a few weeks to two years of coursework. Certificates help prepare individuals for different middle-skill jobs, which require more than a high school diploma but less than an associate's degree. Individuals can then build on this initial short-term credential to earn other certificates and degrees.

The traditional structure of postsecondary education in the United States has been particularly inadequate for low-income individuals, individuals of color, and older adults. For many, the thought of pursuing a bachelor's degree might seem unrealistic or unattractive given the substantial financial costs and the competing demands from work and personal responsibilities. Many individuals who do choose to pursue a degree drop out before completing any credential. Ideally, stackable credentials can increase enrollment and completion rates for historically underserved populations and reduce inequities by providing more-flexible programs with multiple on-ramps and off-ramps and additional opportunities to mix work and education.

There are, however, concerns that stackable credentials might not advance equity for low-income individuals and other underserved populations. Many short-term credentials lead to jobs with low earnings and limited wage growth, and individuals must go on to earn additional credentials to achieve a middle-class income. Prior research has shown that among certificate-completers, individuals of color and older learners might be somewhat less likely to stack credentials and might see smaller earnings when they do stack, yet there is little evidence on socioeconomic disparities in stacking (Bohn, Jackson and McConville, 2019; Bohn and McConville, 2018; Daugherty and Anderson, 2021; Daugherty et al., 2020; Giani and Fox, 2016; Meyer, Bird, and Castleman, 2020). In addition, there have been no efforts to investigate which factors might be contributing to inequities within stackable credential pipelines. To ensure that stackable credentials advance equity, it is critical to understand why certain groups of individuals are less likely to stack credentials and see earnings gains, and important to identify ways to strengthen stackable credential programs to ensure that low-income individuals can earn and stack credentials that offer value in the labor market.

This report contributes additional evidence on equity in stackable credential pipelines in two areas. First, given limited evidence on socioeconomic disparities in credential-stacking and employment outcomes, we examine patterns in stacking and outcomes for low-income students and middle- and high-income students, who we grouped together for this comparison. Second, we conduct deeper inquiry into four possible systems-level barriers that might obstruct opportunities to stack credentials and experience earnings gains for historically underserved populations in stackable credential pipelines: (1) limited opportunities to stack credentials in some fields, (2) limited opportunities to stack credentials in some institutions, (3) insufficient information and resources to identify and stack credentials of value, and (4) challenges moving from noncredit to credit programs. We examined evidence from Colorado and Ohio, two states that are actively engaged in initiatives to scale stackable credentials. We used a mixed methods approach, drawing on descriptive analysis of administrative data and qualitative analysis of interview and survey data with key stakeholders.

We start by providing additional background on stackable credentials and the two states where the research took place and by describing how the study aims to contribute to evidence on stackable credentials and equity in Chapter 2. We then provide a brief overview of the data and our approach to building evidence on equity in stackable credential pipelines in Chapter 3. Our findings are broken into two chapters. Chapter 4 examines evidence on whether patterns in credential-stacking and labor market outcomes differ for low-income individuals relative to middle- and high-income individuals. Chapter 5 examines evidence on our four potential systems-level barriers to stacking. We conclude with a discussion of what these results mean for the stackable credentials movement and the states participating in the work in Chapters 6 and 7.

CHAPTER 2

Background and Study Aims

Initiatives that support the expansion of nondegree credentials and opportunities to stack credentials are playing an important role in transforming the national postsecondary landscape and are a priority for Colorado and Ohio. There is a growing body of evidence on stackable credentials and their implications for equity. This chapter provides a brief overview of the context in which our study took place.

National Efforts to Scale Nondegree, Stackable Credentials

For 15 years, the prevalence of nondegree credentials (e.g., noncredit and credit certificates) has been rapidly expanding in the U.S. postsecondary system. A 2022 report noted that there are more than 1 million unique credentials offered in the United States (Credential Engine, 2022). Many of these credentials are short-term, nondegree credentials, including credit-bearing certificates and noncredit certificates awarded by community colleges and universities and noncredit credentials offered by state-funded technical schools and a wide variety of training providers that are not accredited postsecondary institutions (e.g., bootcamps, industry certification bodies). Data from the National Center for Education Statistics (de Brey et al., 2019) show that the number of certificates awarded annually in the United States peaked at just over 1 million in 2010 and 2011, and that number has declined slightly since.

Stackable credential initiatives call on institutions to arrange these nondegree credentials into sequences of programs and credentials that offer different levels and types of training that might be needed throughout a career, commonly referred to as *career pathways*. For example, institutions might embed short-term certificate programs into longer-term programs so that individuals can continue to earn longer-term certificates and applied associate's and bachelor's degrees after the initial short-term certificate without having to retake technical coursework (Center for Occupational Research and Development, 2021; Wilson, 2016). Institutions might also attempt to embed industry credentials within educational programs so that students can earn industry credentials and educational certificates simultaneously (Center for Occupational Research and Development, 2021). And while some initiatives have focused on building stackable programs within a single institution, articulation agreements and partnerships between institutions to co-design pathways have also grown in popularity. These policies and practices expand opportunities for students to stack credentials across institutions (Ganzglass, 2014).

Several factors have likely contributed to the growing popularity of nondegree credentials and stackable credential pathways. Changes in the economy and the skill requirements for different occupations have led to the growth of middle-skill jobs, jobs that require education and training beyond a high school diploma but short of a degree (Holzer, 2015; Kennedy, Fry, and Funk, 2021). In addition, the U.S. Department of Labor has engaged in efforts to expand the number of individuals earning credentials through such programs as Career Pathways, the Workforce Investment Act, the National Emergency Act, and Trade Adjustment Assistance to provide funding and guidance to states and institutions. For example, between 2011 and 2018, the Trade Adjustment Assistance Community College and Career Training (TAACCCT) grant program provided education and training institutions across the country with more than $2 billion in competitive grants to build stackable credentials in fields such as manufacturing, health care, and IT (Blume et al., 2019). States have also provided a greater level of funding for nondegree programs and stackable credential development through grants to institutions that cover the cost of program design, increased state reimbursement to institutions for certificate programs, experimentation with the expansion of Pell Grants to short-term programs, and state financial aid programs that cover the student costs of short-term programs. Organizations and intermediaries (e.g., National Skills Coalition, the Council for Adult and Experiential Learning, Education Strategy Group, and the Center for Occupational Research and Development) also provide guidance and technical assistance that encourages the arrangement of programs and credentials into stackable credential and career pathways.

Designing stackable credential pathways involves many different organizations and stakeholder groups. In the public education system, high schools, technical schools, community colleges, and regional universities all play a role in awarding different types of credentials; ideally these institutions are working together to build pathways that span a single institution. There are also broad networks of private training providers and credentialing bodies that award credentials. Stackable credential initiatives call on colleges and other education and training providers to closely engage with industry to better align the structure of credentialing with workforce needs and ensure that the credentials awarded will be perceived as valuable by employers and support career advancement for individuals. Legislators, state agencies, and college systems can support stackable credential efforts through funding, policy, program approval processes, technical assistance, and other centralized resources. Within education and training institutions, there are also a broad variety of staff who must contribute to stackable program development; these individuals span noncredit and credit departments within institutions and include administrators, faculty, advisors, and other support staff.

The Context for Stackable Credentials in Colorado and Ohio

The Colorado Department of Higher Education oversees 13 universities and 15 community colleges, and according to the agency's website, these institutions enrolled more than 220,000 undergraduates in fall 2021. All but two of the community colleges are organized under the Colorado Community College System (CCCS). The Colorado Department of Education also oversees three public technical schools. The Ohio Department of Higher Education (ODHE) oversees 14 universities, 23 community colleges, and 50 technical colleges enrolling 449,982 undergraduate students in fall 2021. Ohio community colleges all operate independently (so might be somewhat less coordinated than in the CCCS), although they receive support from the Success Center for Ohio Community Colleges and Ohio Association of Community Colleges.

Technical schools provide noncredit certificates; these certificate programs typically prepare individuals to sit for industry certification and licensing exams or to directly enter the workforce. The network of Ohio Technical Centers (OTCs) award tens of thousands of "clock hour" certificates each year to students. OTCs were initially overseen by the Ohio Department of Education (the kindergarten-through-grade-12 agency) but moved under ODHE in 2012. Being housed under the postsecondary education agency offered more opportunities for these institutions to coordinate and align programs with colleges (although the technical college sites also maintain strong alignment across adult training and high school programs). In contrast, technical schools are a somewhat smaller part of Colorado's system. Community colleges in Colorado and Ohio provide both noncredit and credit programs and credentials, while universities largely provide credit-bearing credentials. In both states, lines between different types of institutions are increasingly blurred as regional universities expand their set of applied programs and community colleges expand their noncredit and applied bachelor's degree programs.

Efforts to scale stackable credentials in Colorado and Ohio are part of a national movement. Ohio was at the forefront of stackable-credential efforts as one of the first states to call for stackable credentials through legislation in 2007. Both states have substantial numbers of middle-skill jobs and are looking to expand stackable credential pathways in key workforce areas, including advanced manufacturing, energy, information technology (IT), and health care. To meet these workforce needs, both states are engaged in efforts to organize high school career and technical education coursework and workforce development efforts around career pathways, and community colleges in both states have engaged in Guided Pathways efforts.[1] Both states participate in foundation-funded networks that provide technical assistance around identifying non-degree credentials of value and ensuring that the credentials lead to good jobs and opportunities to stack credentials, with equity as a focal aim of these efforts. Colorado passed legislation in 2022 calling for the scaling of stackable credential pathways in five high-demand areas and is engaged in a U.S. Department of Education-funded project called "Credential As You Go" that supports states in scaling stackable credential systems. Institutions in both states have seen increased funding for nondegree programs through changes to formula funding, including funding to institutions to cover the cost of short-term programs that are not eligible for financial aid. Both states are pursuing statewide articulation frameworks that establish common standards for articulation across institutions at different levels, although Ohio is slightly further along in implementing statewide articulation agreements that award credit for noncredit learning.

This study builds on prior research on stackable credentials in Ohio. Analysis of program data showed substantial growth in certificate programs offered in health care, IT, and manufacturing and engineering technology (MET) (Daugherty and Anderson, 2021). According to program approval data for certificate programs in Ohio, these programs are being embedded in degree programs (ranging from 39 percent of health care certificate programs to 64 percent of IT certificate programs), aligned with industry credentials (ranging from 59 percent of MET certificate programs to 71 percent of IT certificate programs), and tied to bilateral articulation agreements (ranging from 38 percent of IT certificate programs to 62 percent of health care certificate programs) (Daugherty and Anderson, 2021). We found that when institutions offer more programs within a narrow field, students are more likely to go on to earn additional credentials (Anderson and Daugherty, 2023). In student-level data, we found large percentages of certificate-earning students going on to stack credentials, and those who did so went on to see improved earnings (Daugherty and Anderson, 2021; Daugherty et al., 2020).

Evidence on Stackable Credentials and Equity

One of the proposed benefits of stackable credential programs is that they might offer new on-ramps into postsecondary education for historically underserved populations (e.g., Austin et al., 2012; Center for Occupational Research and Development, 2018; Wilson, 2016). Yet, so far, there is limited evidence on how stackable credentials are helping to advance equity in postsecondary education. Ohio and national data suggest that certificate-earners are more likely than degree-earners to be individuals of color or to be older learners (e.g., Daugherty et al., 2020; National Center for Education Statistics, 2021a; National Center for Education Statistics, 2021b). For example, individuals of color accounted for 49 percent of all certificates earned in the United States in 2019 and 2020 versus 39 percent of bachelor's degrees earned (National Center for Education Statistics, undated-b; National Center for Education Statistics, undated-c). Research indicates that individuals earning certificates begin with relatively low wages and can see meaningful earnings gains from certifi-

---

[1] Guided Pathways is a whole-college redesign model designed to help all students explore, choose, plan, and complete programs aligned with their career and education goals efficiently and affordably.

cates, although these gains are somewhat lower than the gains in earnings from degrees (see, for example, Bahr, 2016; Bahr et al., 2015; Belfield and Bailey, 2017; Bettinger and Soliz, 2016; Minaya and Scott-Clayton, 2022). Analyses of state administrative data have shown that going on to earn additional postsecondary credentials (or stacking credentials) after a certificate can increase wages (Bohn, Jackson, and McConville, 2019; Daugherty and Anderson, 2021; Meyer, Bird, and Castleman, 2020), while an analysis of national survey data did not find evidence that stacking credentials was associated with improved labor market outcomes (Bailey and Belfield, 2017b).

Several studies have examined subgroup differences in patterns of credential-stacking and subsequent returns to earnings and find disparities in the types of credentials being earned, rates of stacking, and earnings gains from stacking across student groups. For example, California data indicate lower rates of stacking and lower returns to credentials for certificate-earning students who were older, male, or students of color (Bohn, Jackson, and McConville, 2019; Bohn and McConville, 2018). In Ohio, older certificate-earners and male certificate-earners were also less likely to stack credentials and saw smaller earning gains, but the racial and ethnic patterns were different (Daugherty and Anderson, 2021; Daugherty et al., 2020). In Ohio, there were not large disparities in rates of stacking by race and ethnicity (Daugherty et al., 2020), and individuals of color saw larger gains from the initial certificate but lower gains from stacking additional credentials (Daugherty and Anderson, 2021). Another study focused on stackable health care programs across states found that Black and Latino students were equally likely to earn short-term certificates but less likely to earn long-term certificates and associate's degrees (Giani and Fox, 2016). This study also examined stacking by income, and findings indicated no clear relationship between Pell Grant eligibility and patterns of credential completion (Giani and Fox, 2016). This was the only study we could find that examined patterns of credential-stacking by income, and we are unaware of any studies that examine how stacking credentials affect earnings for low-income individuals.

Our Contributions to the Evidence

In this report, we aim to address two gaps in the current evidence base on stackable credentials and equity. First, there is limited evidence on how low-income students are stacking credentials and whether credential-stacking is leading to improved labor market outcomes. To fill this gap, we examined whether low-income certificate-earners were more or less likely to stack credentials. We also examined whether low-income certificate-earners stacked credentials vertically or horizontally, within the same field or in different fields, and in staggered or simultaneous fashions. Distinguishing between vertical and horizontal stacking and within-field versus out-of-field stacking is important because prior evidence suggests that these patterns of stacking are associated with stronger labor market return (Daugherty and Anderson, 2021; Meyer, Bird, and Castleman, 2020). While there is limited prior evidence on simultaneous versus staggered stacking, stakeholders have raised concerns about practices such as "autoawarding" credentials or "degree mining," practices in which institutions might be embedding and awarding multiple simultaneous credentials within programs that offer limited independent value to individuals. Finally, we examined whether stacking credentials improves labor market outcomes for low-income individuals and closes earnings gaps relative to middle- and high-income individuals.

Although the existing literature on credential-stacking describes subgroup differences in credentials earned and labor market outcomes, little work has been done to explore which factors might be driving inequities within stackable credential pipelines. Using mixed methods evidence, we examined four potential systemic barriers within stackable credential pipelines that might disadvantage low-income individuals and other historically underserved populations. Table 2.1 provides an overview of the four potential barriers to equity in stackable credential pipelines that we examined in the study.

Barrier One: Limited Opportunities to Stack Credentials in Some Fields

Prior research indicates that rates of stacking vary widely across fields of study (Bohn, Jackson, and McConville, 2019; Daugherty et al., 2020). Some of this variation might reflect differences in the opportunities to stack credentials in these fields. Certain fields could lend themselves to stackable credentials because of the specific needs of the workforce (Cleary and Van Noy, 2014; U.S. Department of Education, 2021). For example, IT is a field where the required skill sets rapidly evolve and constant reskilling and credentialing is a necessity to remain employed. In nursing, the call for nurses with bachelor's degrees to be the standard within the health care field at many hospitals led to a need for stackable programs that could quickly upskill the existing population of nurses who held associate's degrees. In fields in which the need for upskilling or reskilling (and credit-bearing credentials more broadly) are less acute, we might anticipate fewer opportunities for stacking. Child care is an example of a field where licensing standards might regulate the credentials an individual must hold. In addition to workforce trends, there might be variation across different fields in whether the instructors and administrators overseeing education and training learn about and adopt initiatives that support credential-stacking, such as articulation agreements, the embedding of industry credentials into credit-bearing programs, and the mapping and alignment of short-term and longer-term programs into pathways.

The programs and credentials offered within a field are just one factor driving opportunities to stack. Even when stackable programs exist, barriers to movement between programs can shape the opportunities individuals have to stack. For example, some health care degree programs have rigorous entry requirements that act as barriers to entry for certain individuals (Bennett et al., 2021; Schmidt and MacWilliams, 2011), and these programs might accept only small portions of credit from the shorter-term credential (Klein-Collins, 2011).

Prior research on credential-stacking suggests that there is substantial sorting of different types of students across different fields of study according to race/ethnicity, gender, and age (Bohn, Jackson, and McConville, 2019; Daugherty et al., 2020; Giani and Fox, 2017). The stacking literature indicates that historically underserved populations end up disproportionately stacking credentials in certain fields of study; for example, health care credentials, which often generate the highest returns, are more frequently completed by younger, White women in California and Ohio (Bohn, Jackson, and McConville, 2019; Daugherty et al., 2020). Little is known about the sorting of low-income individuals into different fields of study, but if these individuals end up in fields with few stackable programs and limited returns from stacking credentials, then they will face systemic barriers to equity within stackable credential pipelines.

To build a better understanding of how opportunities to stackable credential programs across different fields might contribute to equity, we built evidence in several areas (see Table 2.1). First, we examined whether field of study varied for low-income certificate-completers and middle- and high-income certificate-completers. We then examined whether low-income students earned certificates and degrees in fields with lower stacking rates. Second, we described some of the factors that might be hindering the adoption of and access to stackable credential opportunities in some fields, according to key stakeholder perspectives. Finally, we gathered stakeholder input on policy and practice solutions for addressing those barriers.

Barrier Two: Limited Opportunities to Stack Credentials in Some Institutions

Institutions often vary in terms of the programs and credentials that are offered and the degree to which these programs are built to be stackable (Anderson and Daugherty, 2023; Bohn and McConville, 2018; Daugherty and Anderson, 2021; Giani and Fox, 2017). Some of the variation in programs offered across institutions might be driven by differences in regional workforce demands (Cleary and Van Noy, 2014; Center for Occupational Research and Development, 2021). This variation could be desirable, because institutions should

TABLE 2.1

An Overview of the Four Systems-Level Barriers to Equity in Stackable Credential Pipelines

Barrier	What We Know from the Literature	What We Examine in This Report

Limited opportunities to stack credentials in some fields	• Rates of stacking vary widely across fields of study
	• Many factors might contribute to variation across fields, such as labor market demands, variation in adoption of stackable practices (e.g., embedding programs, articulation agreements), and administrative or enrollment requirements that act as barriers to entry
	• Individuals with different characteristics (e.g., age, gender, race/ethnicity) often complete credentials in different fields
		• Whether low-income individuals end up completing credentials in different fields than middle- and high-income individuals
		• Whether low-income students end up completing credentials in fields with low rates of stacking
		• Stakeholder perspectives on
		  – factors that might limit stackable program development in some fields
		  – policies and practices that might support stackable program expansion across fields

Limited opportunities to stack credentials in some institutions	• Programs offered across institutions vary widely
	• Many factors might contribute to variation across institutions, such as labor market demands, resources, and variation in adoption of applied, nondegree programs and stackable practices (e.g., embedding programs, articulation agreements)
	• Low-income individuals are often constrained to local institutions
	• Most stacking takes place within a single institution
	• Certificate-earners who attend institutions with more credentials in a field are more likely to reenroll and stack credentials
		• Whether rates of stacking vary across institutions
		• Whether low-income individuals end up completing credentials in institutions that have low rates of stacking
		• Stakeholder perspectives on
		  – factors that might limit stackable program development in some institutions
		  – policies and practices that might support stackable program expansion across institutions

Insufficient information to identify and stack credentials of value	• Given variation across fields and institutions, stackable pathways can be complex for individuals to understand
	• Individuals need information on how credentials stack and how they improve job opportunities (i.e., their value)
	• Low-income individuals might face constraints (e.g., limited time, different networks) that increase their need for clear information on programs and credential value
	• Clear information on stackable credentials is often limited
		• Which fields see the highest returns from credential-stacking
		• Whether low-income individuals end up completing credentials in fields that had low returns
		• Stakeholder perspectives on
		  – factors that hinder the information individuals have on stackable programs and credential value
		  – policies and practices that might support improved information to support decisionmaking

Challenges moving from noncredit to credit programs	• Stackable credential pipelines aim to offer individuals opportunities to stack both credit and noncredit credentials
	• Students face several barriers moving from noncredit to credit programs, including siloes between noncredit and credit departments, a lack of clear articulation policies, and program requirements (e.g., general education, applications) that limit movement between systems
	• Relatively few students who start in noncredit programs go on to earn credit-bearing credentials
		• Whether low-income individuals are more likely to complete noncredit credentials
		• Whether there are differences in the types of stacking for individuals who start with noncredit credentials
		• Stakeholder perspectives on
		  – factors that hinder stacking of noncredit and credit credentials
		  – policies and practices that might support improved movement between noncredit and credit programs

not be creating programs unless there are jobs for the students who complete those programs. Resource constraints at certain institutions might also play an important role, because it can be costly to build new programs and cover the costs of the faculty and equipment that support such programs. Institutions engage in a wide variety of efforts to build stackable programs (e.g., mapping and embedding credentials, establishing articulation agreements), and the rate at which institutions adopt these approaches might vary.

The literature suggests that what is offered within an individual's local institution is important in shaping an individual's set of education and training options, because individuals often attend institutions close to their homes; this is particularly true for low-income individuals (Klasik, Blagg, and Pekor, 2018; Mattern and Wyatt, 2009). Evidence also suggests that most stacking takes place within a single institution (Daugherty et al., 2020), and when institutions offer more programs, their certificate-earning students are more likely to go on to stack credentials (Anderson and Daugherty, 2023).

We did not find any prior literature documenting whether low-income individuals attend institutions that offer different programs or fewer stackable opportunities. To build evidence on this, we examined the degree to which rates of stacking vary across institutions, and we explored whether low-income individuals are concentrated in institutions with lower stacking rates. We then drew on the perspectives of key stakeholders to understand what factors might be hindering the adoption of stackable credential opportunities in some institutions and whether there are policy and practice solutions for ensuring broad adoption of stackable credentials across institutions.

Barrier Three: Insufficient Information to Identify and Stack Credentials of Value

As described above, the opportunities to stack credentials might vary widely across fields and institutions, leading to a complex web of programs and credential options for individuals to navigate. The value of these programs in terms of increased earnings vary widely across fields and credential types; for example, research shows that stacking health care credentials, stacking to the degree level (i.e., vertical stacking), and stacking within the same field consistently lead to the highest gains in earnings (Bohn, Jackson, and McConville, 2019; Daugherty and Anderson, 2021; Meyer, Bird, and Castleman, 2020). As a result, which fields and credentials individuals choose to stack are important. Individuals need clear information on stackable credentials to identify *credentials of value*, those that offer longer-term opportunities for education and career growth.

High-quality information and career counseling can shape decisions about institutions and programs (Duke-Benfield et al., 2019; Hoxby and Turner, 2015; Karp, 2013). To inform individuals about programs, institutions might offer online and hard-copy resources and provide guidance (e.g., advising, career services, information on enrollment and faculty) through conversations between individuals and college staff. However, the informational resources available to individuals on the quality and stackability of nondegree programs are often insufficient (Duke-Benfield et al., 2019), and career exploration and advising on program selection is often limited in community colleges (Karp, 2013; Jenkins, Lahr, and Mazzariello, 2021; Rutschow, Tessler, and Lewy, 2021). Many individuals enter college with little sense of how to link academic and career plans (Karp, 2013). Accessible information on stackable programs and their value might be particularly important for low-income individuals who face time constraints and need to make more-difficult decisions about whether enrollment is feasible given financial, work, and life circumstances (Karp, 2013; Van Noy et al., 2016).

We examined informational resources as a barrier to equity in stackable credential pipelines in several ways (see Table 2.1). We first looked at variation in earnings gains across fields and examined whether low-income individuals more commonly ended up in fields that offer limited economic prospects. We then drew on the perspectives of key stakeholders to understand which factors might be contributing to insufficient information and resources for individual decisionmaking. Finally, we explored stakeholder perspectives on opportunities for policy and practice solutions that might improve the accessibility of stackable credential information.

Barrier Four: Challenges Moving from Noncredit to Credit Programs

The vision for stackable credential pipelines is that they offer opportunities to stack a wide variety of college credit–bearing and noncredit credentials (e.g., certificates, degrees, licenses, certifications). However, the literature suggests that individuals face substantial barriers moving between noncredit and credit programs to stack different types of credentials. Some of the issues hindering noncredit-to-credit stacking include siloes between noncredit and credit departments (Buckwalter and Maag, 2019; Education Strategy Group, 2020; Jacoby, 2019; Jenkins, Lahr, and Mazzariello, 2021; Rutschow, Tessler, and Lewy, 2021), administrative barriers to articulating credit (Buckwalter and Maag, 2019; Ganzglass, 2014; Jacoby, 2019; Price and Sedlack, 2018), and general education and selective enrollment that creates barriers to entry and movement through programs (Duke-Benfield et al., 2019; Rosen and Molina, 2019; Rutschow, Tessler, and Lewy, 2021).

Lower-income individuals are particularly likely to start with noncredit training and can be disproportionately affected by barriers to moving from these credential programs into credit-bearing programs (Buckwalter and Maag, 2019; Education Strategy Group, 2020; Rutschow, Tessler, and Lewy, 2021; Xu and Ran, 2020). Research suggests that very few students from noncredit programs go on to complete credit-bearing credentials (Bahr et al., 2022; Xu and Ran, 2020). To build additional evidence on noncredit-to-credit movement, we examined the degree to which low-income individuals were concentrated in noncredit programs and assessed rates and types of stacking for those who start with noncredit certificates and those who start with credit certificates. We also drew on the perspectives of key stakeholders to understand what factors might be contributing to low rates of noncredit-to-credit stacking, and whether there are policy and practice solutions that might improve opportunities to stack different types of credentials.

CHAPTER 3

Our Study Approach

As outlined in the previous chapter, we aimed to build evidence on stackable credentials and equity in two areas: (1) determining whether low-income individuals stack credentials and experience improved labor market outcomes to the same degree as middle- and high-income individuals and (2) understanding how four potential systemic barriers within stackable credential pipelines might disadvantage low-income individuals and other historically underserved populations. We took a mixed methods approach to building this evidence; we drew on administrative data analysis for both aims and conducted qualitative analysis and a scan of websites to contribute to the second aim. This chapter provides a brief overview of our study approach and the data sources that contributed to our work. A more-detailed discussion of the data and methods for the study can be found in the appendix.

A Framework Guiding Our Exploration of Potential Systemic Barriers to Equity

Prior to engaging in research, we developed a framework for equity in stackable credential pipelines to structure and focus our research. The draft framework included a description of each of our four potential systemic barriers to equity, evidence from the literature related to the barrier, and a list of exploratory questions we hoped to answer through the study. Table 2.1 is a condensed version of the framework. We shared this draft framework with our advisory group and four experts in the field and revised the framework according to their feedback.

Descriptive Analysis of Administrative Data

The CCCS and the Ohio Longitudinal Data Archive (OLDA) provided the data used to conduct the quantitative analytical components of this study. The data included administrative records of individuals' enrollments and credential attainment and matched records from the National Student Clearinghouse (NSC), which enabled us to track postsecondary enrollment and stacking outside the respective systems. The data also included matched records from each state's unemployment insurance (UI) database.

Our primary sample consisted of individuals who earned their first-ever observed short- or long-credit certificate from one of 13 CCCS colleges or one of 23 Ohio community colleges between July 1, 2006, and June 30, 2015. These individuals might have previously earned an associate's degree or a higher-level credential. We further limited our sample to individuals who were between the ages of 20 and 64 when they earned their first certificates, were Colorado or Ohio residents, and were never dual-enrolled high school students. More information on the sample is provided in the appendix.

Using data from Ohio, we constructed a separate sample to analyze stacking from noncredit-to-credit–bearing credentials. This sample was composed of individuals who either earned a first noncredit clock-hour certificate (also known as an *industry credential*) from an OTC or a short- or long-credit certificate from a community college between July 1, 2016, and June 30, 2017. Data issues for OTCs prior to 2016 restricted our analysis to students awarded first certificates in this more-limited time frame. We did not have data on non-credit credentials awarded by community colleges, universities, or private providers in Ohio, nor did we have any data on noncredit credentials from Colorado.

To determine a certificate-earner's income status, we relied primarily on UI wage records. Using these records, we first summed each certificate-earner's income between nine and 12 quarters prior to the quarter in which the individual attained a first certificate, thus obtaining a year of income in a time frame in which the individual was unlikely to be enrolled in college. An individual was classified as *low-income* if their wages in this period were below 200 percent of the Federal Poverty Level (FPL), and *middle- and high-income* if their wages were at or above 200 percent of the FPL. This threshold has been used to distinguish between low-income and middle-income brackets in prior research on credential-stacking (e.g., Bohn, Jackson, and McConville, 2019; Daugherty and Anderson, 2021) and in research on such topics as income volatility (e.g., Heflin, 2016; Maag et al., 2017). In Colorado, if a certificate-earner did not have wage records for the required time frame, we turned to financial aid application information. Individuals without wage records but with financial aid application information were classified as low-income if their Expected Family Contribution (EFC) was at or below the threshold for receiving a Pell Grant and as middle- and high-income otherwise. We did not have comparable financial aid application information for individuals in Ohio.

Figure 3.1 disaggregates the primary sample of individuals who earned short- or long-credit certificates by state and income status. In both states, more than half of certificate-earners were low-income. There were fewer individuals of unknown income status in Colorado than in Ohio because we were able to draw on multiple data sources for Colorado.

In Table 3.1, we provide demographic information about our sample, disaggregated by income status. Notably, most certificate-earners were age 25 or older, but low-income certificate-earners tended to be younger than middle- and high-income certificate-earners. Across states, about 40 percent of low-income certificate-

FIGURE 3.1

Certificate-Earners' Income Status, by State

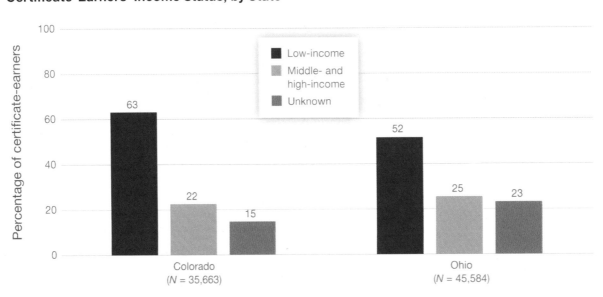

SOURCE: Authors' calculations using data from the CCCS and OLDA.

NOTE: The sample included students who earned their first certificate from a CCCS or Ohio community college between July 1, 2006, and June 30, 2015. Percentages might not sum to 100 because of rounding.

earners were age 20–24, compared with less than 10 percent of middle- and high-income certificate-earners. This is not necessarily surprising, because income typically increases with age.

Additionally, though certificate-earners in both states largely identified as White, greater percentages of low-income certificate-earners in both states identified as Asian, Black or African American, or Hispanic or Latino than did middle- and high-income certificate-earners. Women were disproportionately represented among low-income certificate-earners in Colorado, and men were disproportionately represented in Ohio.

TABLE 3.1

Certificate-Earners' Background Characteristics, by State and Income

	Colorado		Ohio	
	Low-Income Certificate-Earners	Middle- and High-Income Certificate-Earners	Low-Income Certificate-Earners	Middle- and High-Income Certificate-Earners
Age				
20–24	37.8%	10.4%	40.3%	3.9%
25–29	22.9%	20.0%	22.0%	17.1%
30–39	21.5%	34.4%	20.7%	34.8%
40–49	11.5%	21.0%	11.3%	27.0%
50–64	6.4%	14.3%	5.7%	17.2%
Mean	30.2	36.5	29.9	38.8
Race/ethnicity				
Asian	2.4%	2.2%	1.5%	1.0%
Black or African American	3.9%	3.7%	12.1%	13.9%
Hispanic	18.3%	13.2%	1.9%	1.8%
White	67.3%	73.2%	79.3%	78.7%
Other	3.4%	2.9%	2.0%	1.2%
Unknown	4.7%	4.8%	3.3%	3.4%
Gender				
Woman	64.2%	52.3%	34.3%	45.8%
Man	35.8%	47.7%	65.7%	54.2%
Highest prior degree earned				
Bachelor's degree or higher	13.2%	22.6%	1.2%	2.4%
Associate's degree	3.9%	4.0%	6.5%	7.0%
No prior degree	82.9%	73.4%	92.3%	90.6%
N (certificate-earners)	22,448	8,004	23,554	11,539

SOURCE: Authors' calculations using data from the CCCS and OLDA.

NOTE: The sample consisted of students who earned their first certificate from a CCCS or Ohio community college between July 1, 2006, and June 30, 2015. We omitted from the table certificate-earners whose income status was unknown. Percentages might not sum to 100 because of rounding.

About 20 percent of the Colorado sample and 10 percent of the Ohio sample had earned an associate's degree or higher prior to earning their first observed certificate.

Interviews and Focus Groups with Key Stakeholders

We conducted interviews with two types of stakeholders: institutional administrators and faculty and stakeholders who could offer a systems-level or state-level perspective. Across the two groups, we conducted interviews with 20 organizations, including community colleges, technical centers, four-year universities, college systems, and state-level agencies. We selected a sample of institutions that represented a variety of institution types (technical college, community college, university), settings (urban, rural, suburban), and sizes and had varying rates of stacking (high rates in all fields, mixed, low rates in all fields). We focused primarily on institutions that served large populations of Pell Grant–eligible students. We asked to interview individuals who had the deepest familiarity with stackable credential efforts in health care, IT, and manufacturing, but we allowed the institutions to select the individuals who participated in the interviews. To identify interviewees who could offer systems- and state-level perspectives, we relied on a convenience sample of individuals provided by our advisory groups. A more-detailed description of the sample is provided in the appendix.

Data collection was conducted virtually through ZoomGov, a videoconferencing platform. Protocol question topics and questions were organized by the four barriers in the conceptual framework. Analysis of the data was conducted through Dedoose, a qualitative analytic software. We coded the data once for key constructs and then a second time for determining relationships between constructs to develop the main themes that emerged from our research questions.

A Scan of Community College Websites for Stackable Credential Information

To supplement our analysis of administrative data and stakeholder interview and focus group data, we examined websites from a sample of 13 community colleges across Colorado and Ohio to get a better understanding of the types of information on stackable credential programs available to individuals. We focused on information provided on certificate programs and other stackable credentials in three fields: health care, IT, and MET. We assessed the overall comprehensiveness and user-friendliness of each website and the extent to which it offered information on five topics considered important to help individuals make decisions about stacking: (1) course requirements for credentials; (2) learning outcomes for credentials; (3) stackability, as defined by certificates being aligned with industry credentials or embedded into degree programs; (4) career and earnings associated with credentials; and (5) guidance on how to choose a field of study.

Study Limitations

Our study approach had several limitations. First, we did not have data on programs or pathways that institutions or systems might have deemed or designed to be stackable. This means we could not distinguish between certificate-earners who stacked via a pathway intended to be stackable and those who earned two potentially unrelated credentials. Although we were cautious in attributing all the stacking we observed in administrative data to stackable programs, it remains important to understand whether low-income individuals are earning multiple credentials and seeing labor market benefits from doing so.

Our data were also limited in terms of the institutions and credentials captured in the data and in terms of our ability to identify income status for all individuals. We limited our sample to students who received their initial certificates at public community colleges, although we were able to observe stacked credentials earned at any institution included in NSC data. Additionally, we were missing data on a large portion of non-credit credentials; the certificates awarded by OTCs were the only noncredit data reported in state data systems. Although our efforts to triangulate financial aid application data and UI data to identify low-income students helped overcome the limitations of each of these unique data sources, income status could not be determined for nearly one-quarter of Ohio students and nearly one-fifth of Colorado students. Despite these limitations, we provide evidence on a large portion of the credential-stacking that is taking place in these two states.

In terms of the qualitative analysis and website scan, we focused on a subset of institutions and stakeholders, and while we tried to include a diverse sample of institutions, our findings might not represent the perspectives of institutions across the two states. In addition, the perspectives we gathered on the barriers were limited to those held by administrators, faculty, and system leaders; we did not collect data from the students who might experience and understand barriers to stackable credentials differently.

CHAPTER 4

Evidence on Credential-Stacking and Labor Market Outcomes by Income

In this chapter, we draw on administrative data from Colorado and Ohio to assess differences in stacking, types of stacking, and labor market returns from stacking for low-income and middle- and high-income certificate-earners. Table 4.1 presents stacking rates for low-income and middle- and high-income certificate-earners in Colorado and Ohio. We defined *stacking* as earning an additional credential of any level, in any field of study, and at any observable institution within the specified number of years of completing a first certificate. (Stacking in zero years refers to *simultaneous stacking* or earning a second credential on the same date as the first certificate.)

Across all time frames, low-income certificate-earners stacked credentials at higher rates than middle- and high-income certificate-earners. For example, 39 percent of Colorado low-income certificate-earners completed a second credential within three years, compared with 33 percent of middle- and high-income certificate-earners; in Ohio, those figures were 43 percent and 36 percent, respectively. The difference in stacking rates between low-income and middle- and high-income students increased over time.

In Figure 4.1, we disaggregated certificate-earners' pathways based on the level of their first certificate (short or long) and the level of their stacked credential (short-credit certificate, long-credit certificate, associate's degree, or bachelor's degree) for certificate-earners who stacked credentials within three years of their first certificate. Most Colorado stackers initially earned a short-credit certificate (73 percent of low-income

TABLE 4.1

Stacking Rates, by State and Income

	Colorado			Ohio		
	Low-Income	Middle- and High-Income	Difference	Low-Income	Middle- and High-Income	Difference
Percentage of credentials stacked						
In zero years	13.0%	11.5%	1.5%	14.8%	11.9%	2.9%
In one year	25.3%	21.9%	3.4%	30.4%	25.7%	4.7%
In two years	32.9%	27.9%	5.0%	37.7%	31.9%	5.8%
In three years	38.6%	32.8%	5.8%	42.6%	36.0%	6.5%
In four years	42.1%	36.1%	6.0%	45.8%	38.8%	7.0%
N (certificate-earners)	22,448	8,004		23,554	11,539	

SOURCE: Authors' calculations using data from the CCCS and OLDA.

NOTE: The sample consisted of students who earned their first certificate from a CCCS or Ohio community college between July 1, 2006, and June 30, 2015. *Stacking* was defined as earning an additional credential of any level, in any field of study, and at any institution within the specified time frame relative to a student's first certificate. We omitted from the table certificate-earners whose income status was unknown.

FIGURE 4.1

Stacking Pathways, by State and Income

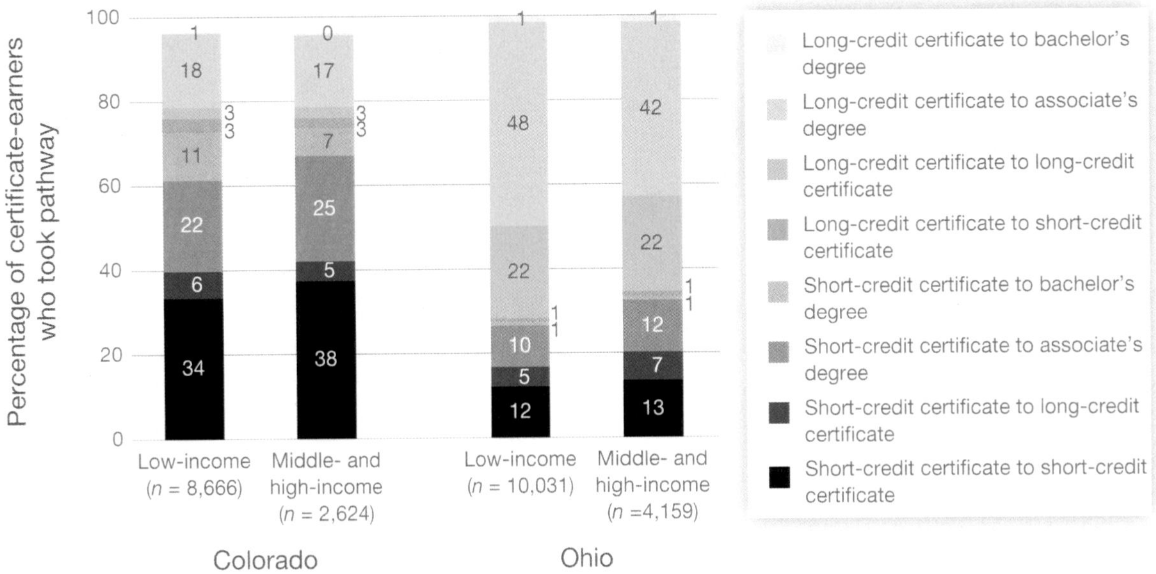

SOURCE: Authors' calculations using data from the CCCS and OLDA.

NOTES: The sample included students who earned their first certificate from a CCCS or Ohio community college between July 1, 2006, and June 30, 2015, and earned an additional credential within three years of their first certificate. We omitted from the table certificate-earners whose income status was unknown. Percentages might not sum to 100 because of rounding, and due to a small number of omitted certificates of unknown length.

stackers and 75 percent of middle- and high-income stackers) while most Ohio stackers initially earned a long-credit certificate (72 percent of low-income stackers and 66 percent of middle- and high-income stackers). In both states, low-income stackers stacked to degrees at higher rates than middle- and high-income stackers. About 53 percent of Colorado and 61 percent of Ohio low-income stackers completed an associate's or bachelor's degree as opposed to 52 percent of middle- and high-income stackers in Colorado and 56 percent in Ohio.

Table 4.2 describes additional characteristics of stackers' stacked credentials, again focusing on those who stacked within three years of the date of their first certificate. Characteristics of interest were whether the stacked credential was vertical (resulting in a higher-level credential) or horizontal (resulting in a certificate of the same or of a lower level compared with the first certificate), whether it was simultaneous stacking (earned on the same date as the first certificate) or staggered stacking (earned at a later date), and whether the stacked credential was in the same field or a different field than the student's first certificate. We defined a *specific* field of study as a field at the four-digit Classification of Instructional Programs (CIP) level and a *broad* field of study as a field at the two-digit CIP level as did Meyer, Bird, and Castleman (2020).

In both states, low-income stackers stacked vertically at higher rates than middle- and high-income stackers (see Table 4.2). Specifically, 58 percent of low-income stackers in Colorado and 65 percent in Ohio stacked vertically compared with 55 percent and 63 percent of middle- and high-income stackers, respectively.

In contrast, patterns of staggered and simultaneous stacking by income differed across states: In Colorado, a greater proportion of low-income stackers earned staggered credentials (compared with Colorado middle- and high-income stackers) whereas in Ohio a greater proportion of low-income stackers (compared with Ohio middle- and high-income stackers) earned simultaneous credentials (see Table 4.2). Most prior research establishing the benefits of credential-stacking has focused on staggered credentials; the finding

TABLE 4.2

Characteristics of Stacked Credentials, by State and Income

	Colorado			Ohio		
	Low-Income	Middle- and High-Income	Difference	Low-Income	Middle- and High-Income	Difference
Vertical	58.2%	54.5%	3.7%	65.1%	62.8%	2.3%
Staggered	66.4%	65.0%	1.4%	65.3%	67.0%	−1.7%
Same specific field	19.4%	17.4%	2.0%	52.5%	52.8%	−0.3%
Same broad field	66.4%	60.2%	6.2%	76.2%	78.4%	−2.2%
n (stackers)	8,666	2,624		10,031	4,159	

SOURCE: Authors' calculations using data from the CCCS and OLDA.

NOTE: The sample consisted of individuals who earned their first certificate from a CCCS or Ohio community college between July 1, 2006, and June 30, 2015, and earned an additional credential within three years of their first certificate. Vertical stacking was defined as earning a higher-level credential, and horizontal stacking was defined as earning an additional credential of the same level. Simultaneous stacking was defined as earning a stacked credential on the same date as the first certificate. A specific field of study was defined at the four-digit CIP level, and a broad field of study was defined at the two-digit CIP level (following Meyer, Bird, and Castleman, 2020). We omitted from the table certificate-earners whose income status was unknown. Percentages might not sum to 100 because of rounding and a small number of omitted certificates of unknown length.

that low-income certificate-earners in Ohio completed simultaneous credentials at higher rates might be problematic if simultaneous stacking does not yield the same benefits as staggered stacking.

Patterns of in-field stacking also varied across states (see Table 4.2). Low-income students in Colorado stacked in the same specific and same broad fields at higher rates than Colorado middle- and high-income stackers, while low-income stackers in Ohio did so at slightly lower rates than Ohio middle- and high-income stackers.

Next, we examined labor market returns from credential-stacking, focusing on the extent to which returns differed for low-income versus middle- and high-income stackers. We also examined whether an individual earned at least a middle-income wage (defined as wages equal to or greater than 200 percent of the FPL), conditional on being employed in a quarter. Results were disaggregated into vertical stacking, horizontal stacking, and no stacking. When interpreting these results, it is important to remember that this analysis is descriptive, and we cannot draw causal conclusions about the effects of stacking on labor market outcomes.

Vertical stacking appeared to be associated with sizeable earnings gains relative to completing just one certificate (Figure 4.2). Within six to eight quarters of completing a first certificate, low-income vertical stackers outearned low-income nonstackers. In Colorado, within 24 quarters, the gaps between low-income vertical stackers and middle- and high-income nonstackers had shrunk from more than $20,000 to just a few thousand dollars. Despite these gains, even low-income vertical stackers continued to earn less than middle- and high-income stackers. Returns from horizontal stacking were notably lower. In Colorado, low-income horizontal stackers earned less than low-income nonstackers throughout the observation window; in Ohio, at the end of the observation period, low-income horizontal stackers only slightly outearned low-income nonstackers.

We also examined the proportion of certificate-earners that achieved middle-income wages and found promising evidence for the potential of credential-stacking to improve outcomes for low-income students (Figure 4.3). At the time of their first certificate, less than 20 percent of low-income vertical stackers in Colorado and Ohio earned at least a middle-income wage; six years later, nearly 80 percent of low-income vertical stackers had attained a middle-income wage. There was a substantial reduction in the gap between low-income and middle- and high-income certificate-earners who had achieved a middle-class wage within 24 quarters in both states. The earnings gains do not look as promising for horizontal stackers; we see little evidence that these credentials led to an improved likelihood of achieving middle-income wages.

FIGURE 4.2

Earnings by State, Income, and Type of Stacking

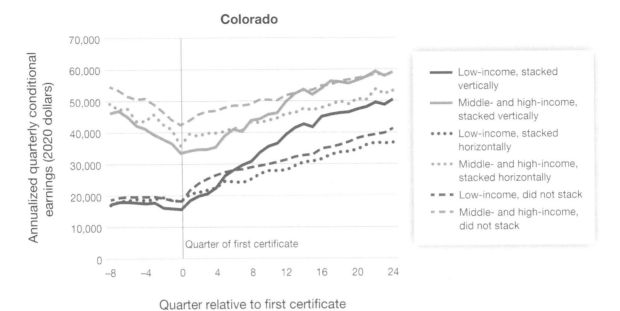

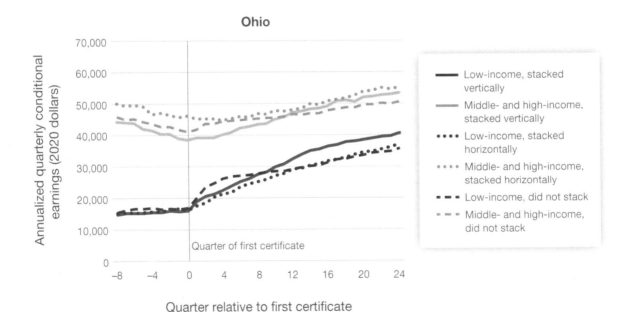

SOURCE: Authors' calculations using data from the CCCS and OLDA.

NOTE: The sample included students who earned their first certificate from a CCCS or Ohio community college between July 1, 2006, and June 30, 2012, conditional on wages > $100 in a quarter. Wages were adjusted to 2020 first-quarter dollars using the Consumer Price Index for all Urban Consumers (CPI-U). Vertical stackers earned an additional, higher-level credential within three years; horizontal stackers earned an additional credential of the same level within three years; and nonstackers did not earn any additional credentials within three years. We omitted from the figure certificate-earners whose income status was unknown.

FIGURE 4.3

FIGURE 4.3

Percentage of Students Who Earn at Least a Middle-Income Wage, by State, Income, and Type of Stacking

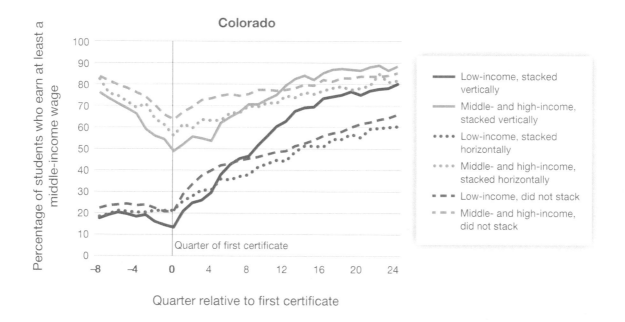

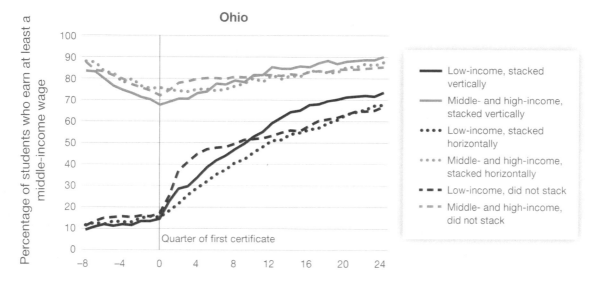

SOURCE: Authors' calculations using data from the CCCS and OLDA.

NOTES: The sample included students who earned their first certificate from a CCCS or Ohio community college between July 1, 2006, and June 30, 2012, conditional on wages > $100 in a quarter. *Middle-income wage* was defined as annualized quarterly earnings > 200 percent of the FPL. Wages were adjusted to 2020 first-quarter dollars using the CPI-U. Vertical stackers earned an additional, higher-level credential within three years; horizontal stackers earned an additional credential of the same level within three years; and nonstackers did not earn any additional credentials within three years. We omitted from the figure certificate-earners whose income status was unknown.

Our findings on credential-stacking and the benefits of stacking for labor market outcomes suggest that credential-stacking can make positive contributions to equity in postsecondary education. Low-income individuals who complete a first certificate stack at higher rates than middle- and high-income certificate-earners commonly stack to a higher-level credential, and they experience earnings gains when they stack vertically. Although the earnings of low-income individuals continued to trail those of their middle- and high-income counterparts, vertical stacking led to substantial reductions in these gaps.

CHAPTER 5

Evidence on Systemic Barriers to Equity in Stackable Credential Pipelines

Examining the evidence on equity within stackable credential pipelines requires us to do more than simply examine patterns by student characteristics, we must dig deeper to understand how stackable credential opportunities across the postsecondary education system might vary in systematic ways that limit opportunities for low-income individuals and other historically underserved communities. We identified four potential barriers to examine in this study, with a focus on barriers that operated at the systems level—barriers that our partners at state agencies and system offices might be best equipped to address. In this chapter, we describe our quantitative and qualitative evidence on each of these barriers. We have combined sections for two of our four barriers (limited opportunities to stack across fields and limited opportunities to stack across institutions) because of the strong overlap in qualitative findings.

Barriers One and Two: Limited Opportunities to Stack in Some Fields and Institutions

Stackable credential pipelines will not be equitable if low-income individuals systematically sort into fields where there are limited stackable credential opportunities or if the local institutions that low-income individuals have access to offer few stackable opportunities. We first examine evidence on these patterns in Colorado and Ohio administrative data. We then describe stakeholder perspectives on the factors that might limit stackable program development in certain fields and institutions, as well as the opportunities for states, systems, and institutions to expand opportunities to stack across fields and institutions.

Evidence from Administrative Data on Low-Income Individuals and Opportunities to Stack by Field

Although low-income certificate-earners stacked at higher rates than their middle- and high-income counterparts, we found that this masked variation in their selection of fields of study and opportunities to stack across fields of study. Several fields with higher proportions of low-income certificate-earners appeared to have fewer opportunities for stacking and fewer opportunities for stacking credentials with arguably more-valuable attributes.

Table 5.1 shows the total number of certificate-earners in the ten most-common fields of study and the percentage of these certificate-earners who were low-income. Fields are listed in order from highest to lowest concentration of low-income certificate-earners in Colorado (although the exact order of fields would differ slightly if listed according to the concentration of low-income certificate-earners in Ohio, most fields would not differ by more than two positions). Across states, low-income certificate-earners were concentrated in education, family and consumer sciences (FCS), mechanics, and, to a lesser extent, nursing and allied health. In contrast, business, IT, MET, and security and protective services had relatively higher concentrations of

TABLE 5.1

Distribution of Low-Income and Middle- and High-Income Certificate-Earners in Ten Common Fields of First Certificate, by State

	Colorado		Ohio	
	Total Certificate-Earners	Low-Income Certificate-Earners (%)	Total Certificate-Earners	Low-Income Certificate-Earners (%)
Culinary and personal services	738	85.2	488	42.6
Mechanics	858	78.8	732	57.1
Education and FCS	1,799	71.2	1,168	58.5
Nursing	9,898	64.5	8,080	60.4
Design and applied arts	388	62.6	1,378	55.7
Allied health	10,632	62.0	12,778	55.7
Business	2,594	59.0	7,011	42.1
Security and protective services	2,718	57.4	1,515	51.3
MET	2,120	56.3	5,455	42.0
IT	1,039	55.1	1,880	39.7

SOURCE: Authors' calculations using data from the CCCS and OLDA.

NOTE: The sample consisted of students who earned their first certificate from a CCCS or Ohio community college between July 1, 2006, and June 30, 2015. The ten fields of study listed here accounted for approximately 90 percent of certificate-earners in Colorado and Ohio, and descriptions of each field are in the appendix. Percentages might not sum to 100 because of rounding and omission of certificate-earners whose income status was unknown.

middle- and high-income certificate-earners. The percentage of certificate-earners who were low-income varied across states for culinary and personal services and for design and applied arts, and these two fields also had low numbers of certificate-earners relative to other fields.

In Figure 5.1, we show the percentage of certificate-earners who were low-income against the stacking rate for the ten most-common fields of first certificate. The size of each circle represents the total number of certificate-earners in the field. In interpreting Figure 5.1, note that more than one-half of certificate-earners in most fields of study were low-income, but some fields still enrolled greater proportions of low-income individuals than others.

Some fields of study—notably education and FCS, mechanics, and, in Ohio, design and applied arts—had both relatively high concentrations of low-income certificate-earners and relatively high stacking rates. Meanwhile, allied health, nursing, and security and protective services had low stacking rates in both states. Culinary and personal services in Colorado was also notable in having a high concentration of low-income certificate-earners and low stacking rates. Fields such as business, IT, and MET had higher stacking rates but lower proportions of low-income certificate-earners.

We next examined whether low-income certificate-earners were concentrated in fields with more limited vertical stacking (Figure 5.2). Because vertical stacking is associated with greater labor market returns, it was important to understand whether low-income certificate-earners have opportunities not only to stack credentials but also to stack in higher-return pathways. In Colorado, low-income certificate-earners were more heavily concentrated in fields with more-limited vertical stacking opportunities. The three fields with the highest concentrations of low-income certificate-earners—education and FCS, mechanics, and culinary and personal services—had some of the lowest percentages of stackers who stacked vertically. Nursing was an

FIGURE 5.1

Concentration of Low-Income Certificate-Earners and Stacking Rates in Common Fields of First Certificate, by State

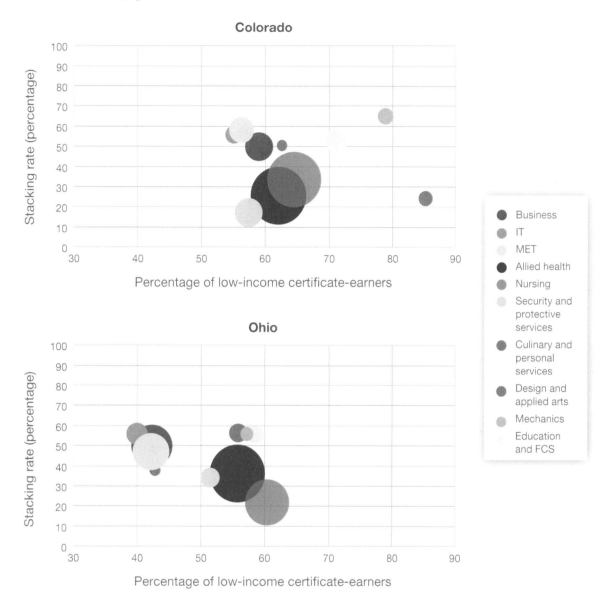

SOURCE: Authors' calculations using data from the CCCS and OLDA.

NOTE: N = 32,784 certificate-earners in Colorado, and N = 40,485 certificate-earners in Ohio. The sample included students who earned their first certificate in one of the 10 listed fields of study from a CCCS or Ohio community college between July 1, 2006 and June 30, 2015. *Stacking* was defined as earning an additional credential of any level, in any field of study, and at any institution within three years of earning a first certificate. The size of the circle represents the relative number of certificate-earners in that field. The ten fields of study listed here accounted for approximately 90 percent of certificate-earners in Colorado and Ohio, and descriptions of each field are in the appendix.

exception, beause it had a medium-to-high proportion of low-income certificate-earners and a higher percentage of stackers who stacked vertically.

The relationship between a field's concentration of low-income certificate-earners and vertical stacking differed somewhat for Ohio. Education and FCS and nursing each had especially high concentrations of low-income certificate-earners and high percentages of stackers who stacked vertically. In contrast, design and applied arts and mechanics had higher concentrations of low-income certificate-earners, but limited per-

FIGURE 5.2

Concentration of Low-Income Certificate-Earners and Prevalence of Vertical Stacking in Common Fields of First Certificate, by State

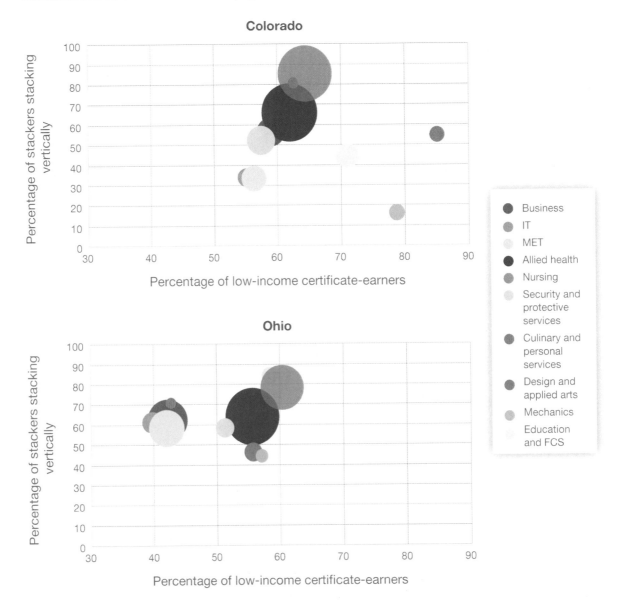

SOURCE: Authors' calculations using data from the CCCS and OLDA.

NOTE: *N* = 32,784 certificate-earners in Colorado, and *N* = 40,485 certificate-earners in Ohio. The sample included students who earned their first certificate in one of the ten listed fields of study from a CCCS or Ohio community college between July 1, 2006, and June 30, 2015. *Vertical stacking* was defined as earning an additional credential of a higher level within three years of earning a first certificate. The size of the circle represents the relative number of certificate-earners in that field. The ten fields of study listed here accounted for approximately 90 percent of certificate-earners in Colorado and Ohio, and descriptions of each field are in the appendix.

centages of stackers vertically stacking. Taken together, these findings suggest that low-income certificate-earners were found in fields with limited vertical stacking opportunities but were also found in fields with more-robust vertical stacking options.

Another type of stacking associated with greater labor market returns was in-field stacking. We thus considered whether low-income certificate-earners might be concentrated in fields with fewer options to earn an additional credential in the same field. As shown in Figure 5.3, in both Colorado and Ohio, most fields had reasonably similar proportions of in-field stacking, regardless of the proportion of low-income certificate-earners. Mechanics, in Colorado, and nursing, in Ohio, were the sole exceptions. These fields had especially high percentages of stackers earning credentials in the same field and higher concentrations of low-income students. Overall, the relationship between a field's concentration of low-income certificate-earners and its percentages of stackers earning both credentials in the same field was negligible, at worst, or positive, at best.

FIGURE 5.3

Concentration of Low-Income Certificate-Earners and Prevalence of In-Field Stacking in Common Fields of First Certificate, by State

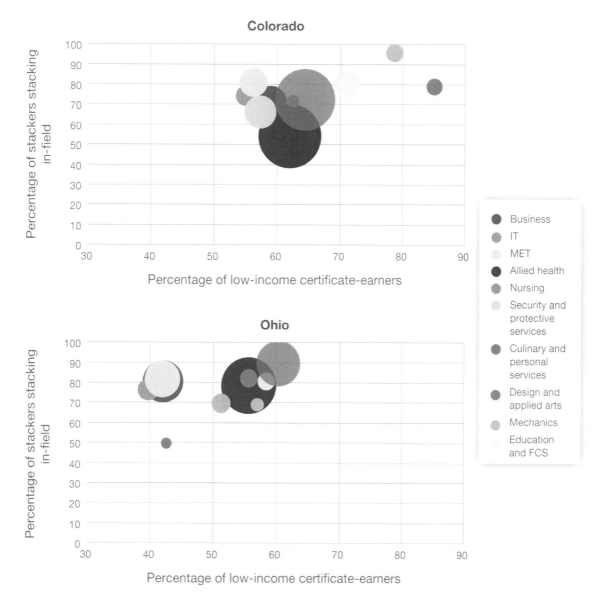

SOURCE: Authors' calculations using data from the CCCS and OLDA.

NOTE: *N* = 32,784 certificate-earners in Colorado, and *N* = 40,485 certificate-earners in Ohio. The sample included students who earned their first certificate in one of the ten listed fields of study from a CCCS or Ohio community college between July 1, 2006, and June 30, 2015. *In-field stacking* was defined as earning an additional credential with the same two-digit Classification of Instructional Programs (CIP) code as the field of first certificate (following Meyer, Bird, and Castleman, 2020). The size of the circle represents the relative number of certificate-earners in that field. The ten fields of study listed here accounted for approximately 90 percent of certificate-earners in Colorado and Ohio, and descriptions of each field are in the appendix.

Evidence from Administrative Data on Low-Income Students and Opportunities to Stack, by Institution

Next, we examined the extent to which stacking and types of stacking varied across institutions. As shown in Figure 5.4, stacking rates varied widely across institutions in both Colorado and Ohio. Stacking rates at CCCS colleges ranged from about 22 percent to about 50 percent. Institution-level stacking rates in Ohio colleges ranged even more widely, between 20 percent and 63 percent.

Although stacking rates varied by institution, we did not find evidence suggesting that low-income certificate-earners were disproportionately concentrated in institutions with lower stacking rates. In fact, in Colorado, institutions with greater shares of low-income certificate-earners also tended to have slightly higher stacking rates, as shown in Figure 5.5. In Ohio, there was no clear relationship between an institution's proportion of low-income certificate-earners and its stacking rate—though there were three small institutions with relatively large shares of low-income certificate-earners and notably lower stacking rates.

There was also mixed evidence as to whether institutions serving large populations of low-income certificate-earners tended to offer credentials and pathways that encourage the types stacking associated with higher earnings gains, such as vertical stacking and in-field stacking. As with overall stacking, in Colorado, institutions with greater proportions of low-income certificate-earners had slightly higher proportions of stackers stacking vertically and in-field. In Ohio, there was no systematic relationship between low-income certificate-earners and vertical or in-field stacking. Because patterns of vertical and in-field stacking were similar to patterns for overall stacking, we omitted these figures.

FIGURE 5.4

Stacking Rates, by State and Institution

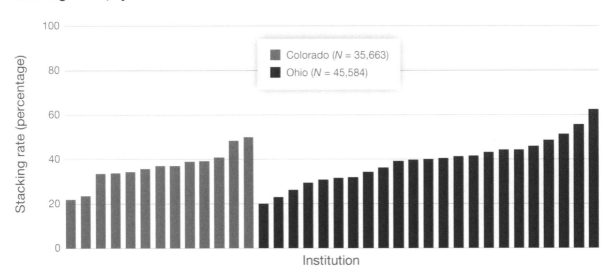

SOURCE: Authors' calculations using data from the CCCS and OLDA.

NOTE: The sample included students who earned their first certificate from a CCCS or Ohio community college between July 1, 2006, and June 30, 2015. *Stacking* was defined as earning an additional credential of any level, in any field of study, and at any institution within three years of earning a first certificate. This is an anonymized representation of the 13 CCCS colleges (orange bars) and the 23 Ohio community colleges (green bars) in this study.

FIGURE 5.5

Relationship Between Institutions' Percentage of Low-Income Certificate-Earners and Stacking Rate, by State

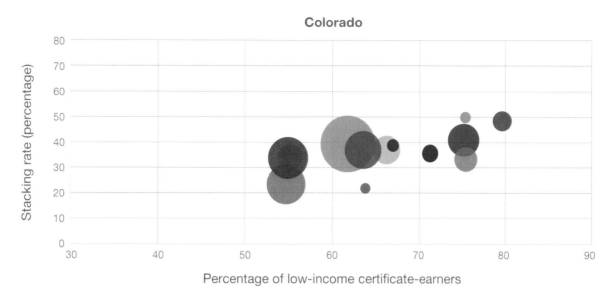

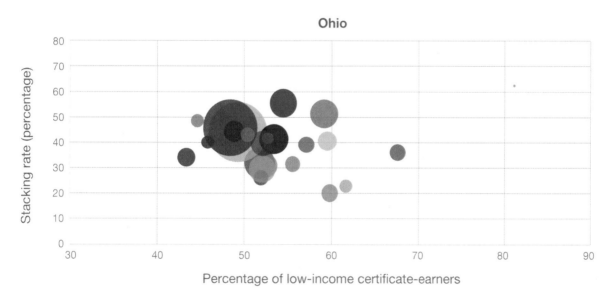

SOURCE: Authors' calculations using data from the CCCS and OLDA.

NOTE: Each circle represents an individual institution. The size of the circle represents the relative number of certificate-earners in an institution. N = 35,663 certificate-earners across 13 CCCS colleges, and N = 45,584 certificate-earners across 23 Ohio community colleges. The sample included students who earned their first certificate from a CCCS or Ohio community college between July 1, 2006, and June 30, 2015. *Stacking* was defined as earning an additional credential of any level, in any field of study, and at any institution within three years of earning a first certificate.

Stakeholder Perspectives on Factors Contributing to Opportunities to Stack in Fields and Institutions

Our findings demonstrate that there is substantial variation in rates of stacking across fields and institutions. Low-income certificate-earners were notably concentrated in certain fields with lower stacking rates and low rates of vertical stacking or in-field stacking, suggesting that a lack of opportunities to stack in some fields might be a barrier to equity for low-income certificate-earners. In contrast, the institutions serving the largest populations of low-income certificate-earners had stacking rates and vertical and in-field stacking rates that were similar to or even greater than the institutions serving fewer low-income certificate-earners.

Institutional staff and system and state leaders reflected on what factors might hinder the development of stackable credential opportunities in some fields and institutions. We describe the six factors mentioned most often in our interviews with participating organizations.

Limited Workforce Needs and Limited Industry Engagement

Across both Colorado and Ohio, state and local economies appear to be the main drivers of stackable credential options. Both states host industries that seek employees with technical knowledge and skills that can often be acquired through short-term certificates. Examples of industries that were mentioned frequently in our conversations include manufacturing, health care (e.g., nursing, phlebotomy), IT, automotive science, and welding. Institutional staff drew on market research, state data, and their working relationships with local companies to determine which fields of study to invest in. According to interviewees, employers' investments in the state will often determine which stackable programs institutions pursue and how they pursue the programs, including identifying the appropriate fields of study. Interviewees described how companies have approached postsecondary institutions to develop a short-term certificate or course for their employees. The needs of local economies will often determine how institutions identify and develop the opportunities for stacking credentials, including the areas and industries with the most need for skilled individuals.

For institutions to understand the needs of local employers, the stakeholders with whom we talked noted that institutions must be deeply engaged with industry in identifying needs for programs and credentials. Cementing that alignment between postsecondary education and industry requires institutions to invest time and resources in developing outreach strategies to engage local companies; these efforts often manifest in the development of field-specific advisory boards that are made up of local industry leaders. Institutions convene their advisory boards several times a year to update them on curricular and student progress and to solicit their insights on industry trends and needs. The effectiveness of advisory boards to offer actionable insights on program design might vary widely because institutions have limited resources for planning. Through our conversations with institutional representatives, we learned that it was common for a single staff or faculty member to lead institution-wide efforts to engage with local employers. Generally, this individual was responsible for reaching out to employers in several fields of study, identifying and convincing industry leaders to participate, managing meeting logistics, and bringing relevant faculty together to develop an agenda that would prompt valuable discussion and feedback from the board. Maintaining effective advisory boards can overtax institutions, many of which are limited in resources. The quality of institutions' engagement with advisory boards can help explain why opportunities for stacking credentials vary widely by institution and field.

Substantial Program Startup Costs

Developing new programs and assembling programs and credentials into stackable pathways requires *startup costs*, an initial investment of time and resources. To start a new program, institutions must conduct market research, compensate faculty and staff for their time and expertise in the planning process, build relations with local businesses, and develop and execute a marketing and outreach plan. In our conversations, institutional representatives expressed challenges in securing the necessary funds to begin the development process, citing limited institutional funds overall. Developing new, stackable programs can be a risky prospect given the challenging financial environment and resource constraints at many institutions.

Burdensome Administrative Processes

The complexity of administrative processes can often play an important role in driving startup costs and can discourage institutions from providing or expanding opportunities to stack credentials. New programs often require approvals by the institution, the state, and accreditors, and, according to some interviewees, this process can often take from six months to a year. Interviewees reported that state approval can be a long and complex process, further delaying program availability. At an institutional level, several departments might impart their own review and requirements before programs can be available to students. The timeline for program development and approval also has implications for how quickly institutions can respond to employer needs, which can vary depending on the industries located near an institution. Interviewees from postsecondary institutions reported that the pace of administrative processes in public postsecondary institutions is not aligned with the needs of workforce development, which can prompt employers to look elsewhere to address their workforce needs. Institutions might only be motivated to identify and invest in fields and opportunities to stack credentials when the benefits clearly outweigh the initial financial and administrative barriers; this might be especially true for industries that are established in the local community around an institution.

Challenges with Faculty Recruitment

Interviewees described how challenges with faculty recruitment can play an important role in limiting the development of new, stackable programs in technical fields. One of the reasons that institutions—especially community colleges and technical centers—across both states struggled to find enough faculty to teach in their programs was competition with private industry in recruiting faculty who teach in fields with stackable options. This competition is especially common for fields such as health care, manufacturing, IT, and welding, where salary potential in the private sector far surpasses what institutions can offer. This might also be true for institutions located in more-rural areas that have access to smaller populations of prospective faculty members. In addition, interviewees from institutions mentioned the difficulty of identifying faculty with the right balance of experience in education and practical work in their field. Often, faculty must have completed advanced coursework in their field. It is also valuable for faculty in these technical fields to have the applied experience that offers a deeper understanding of the work in the field and the ability to facilitate connections with employers willing to bring students on for apprenticeships or full-time work. There are few individuals with this combination of education and experience in technical fields, with shortages being more pronounced in fields and regions where potential faculty have various other job options with high earning potential.

Insufficient Access to Equipment and Instructional Resources

Providing stackable programs is dependent on the availability of the resources necessary for student learning and training. Institutional staff noted the difficulty of purchasing equipment (e.g., for machining) for training, especially as fields change curricular standards and adopt new practices. Faculty from institutions in rural areas mentioned significant distances to the closest training and clinical facilities, which place an additional strain on faculty and student time and resources. Although the coronavirus 2019 (COVID-19) pandemic has pushed institutions to improve delivery of online courses, access to Wi-Fi continues be a barrier for students, especially those from rural areas. Without proper materials, technologies, and facilities, institutions encounter a difficult path toward making stackable options attractive and accessible to students. The anticipated costs to provide students with what they need to pursue short-term certificates and, subsequently, stackable options can discourage institutions from adopting or expanding stackable credentials.

Competition Between Institutions

Postsecondary institutions (technical schools, community colleges, and universities) in both states operate under a relatively decentralized system of postsecondary education. Colorado community colleges are organized under a common system to a greater degree than Ohio community colleges, but institutions in both states often design programs independently. State and institutional representatives reported limited structures for encouraging a level of collaboration across different levels of institutions that could discourage competition between institutions for resources, industry partners, and students. As a result, there are perceptions of inefficiencies in how programs are developed across institutions, such as the duplication of programs in a region or a failure to share promising approaches to building out stackable programs. In addition to competitiveness, there might be cultural barriers within postsecondary education systems related to perceptions of program and institutional quality and the failure of institutions to see each other as partners in a common system. For example, some state leaders and institutional administrators mentioned how technical centers can be perceived as inferior institutions by other institutions in their state. Lastly, this competitive landscape has led some institutions to focus on local needs, especially in regions where particular industries are the strongest, which could drive further variation in opportunities to stack credentials across institutions and fields.

Stakeholder Perspectives on Options to Ensure Stackable Credential Opportunities Across Fields and Institutions

To address the factors contributing to limited stackable credential opportunities in certain fields and institution, the stakeholders we interviewed reflected on different policy and practice solutions. In the following sections, we describe six of their suggested approaches to strengthening stackable opportunities.

Improve Coordination with Industry

Coordination with industry is important to the development of stackable programs. But these efforts can require substantial time and effort, which can affect the effectiveness of partnerships with local employers. State leaders could play a more-significant role in facilitating intentional interaction between postsecondary institutions and industry. Because many institutions are resource constrained, they can benefit from state support in the form of market research on current and emerging industry trends and identification of promising partnerships between institutions and local employers. For example, Colorado produces an annual *Colorado Talent Pipeline Report*, and this report provides evidence on high-growth industries that has been used to inform focus areas for stackable credential development under 2022 legislation (Colorado General Assembly, 2022). State leaders could also consider hosting regional meetings that bring relevant stakeholders together to forge partnerships organically. Having the state lead these efforts enhances the legitimacy of stackable options in the eyes of employers and can encourage their participation. Lastly, state leaders could consider providing supplemental grants that fund activities to promote institution-employer relationships (e.g., advisory boards, codesigning competencies, or apprenticeships) and support the hiring of additional personnel who can manage these activities and future outreach. For example, in Colorado, efforts to strengthen partnerships between employers and institutions are underway through the Opportunity Now Colorado initiative. The $85-million grant program encourages institutions and industry to come together to develop educational programs that align with in-demand and high-paying occupations.

Assist with Startup Costs

Many institutions face challenges covering the startup costs associated with developing new programs. To address this barrier, state leaders could consider a grant initiative that provides seed funding to encourage program development. The initiative could prioritize under-resourced institutions or institutions seeking to develop stackable options in industries with the highest shortages of skilled workers. Colorado has invested around $20 million to help community colleges start or develop their programs; about one-half of that funding has emphasized clean energy and nursing programs. Program development is often led by faculty, who are already inundated with their primary responsibilities of teaching and advising. Many faculty are also on a nine-month contract, which means that they are not required to work during the summer term. Some funding from the state could incentivize faculty to work on program development during the summer, rather than waiting for the academic year to begin.

Improve Administrative Processes

Administrative burden is a major driver of time costs associated with the startup of new programs, and there are ways that the state and institutions can streamline program approval processes to address this burden. Every institution has a distinct process of review, approval, and execution of new academic programs. Some institutional representatives recommended a repository of preapproved templates that could guide new programs and minimize administrative processing time. While state leaders are limited in their capacities to shape internal institutional processes, they can reconsider how their own requirements for program review and approval are barriers to developing stackable options. By helping reduce administrative barriers, the state makes it easier for institutions to more immediately meet industry needs.

Improve the Competitiveness of Institutions for Faculty Recruitment

To address the costs associated with recruiting and retaining faculty in a competitive environment, states could potentially help address the systematic barriers to faculty recruitment in two ways. First, state leaders could consider providing institutions with supplementary funding to improve their competitiveness in faculty recruitment. Funding allocations could prioritize fields with the highest disparities between private industry and instructional salaries or institutions located in more-rural areas of their states. Second, states could consider ways to expand the pool of faculty with the right mix of work experience and education. For example, states could facilitate partnerships with industry that provide more-streamlined opportunities for individuals in the field to become instructors.

Improve Coordination Among Institutions

A lack of coordination among institutions can potentially lead to gaps and duplication in programs offered. State leaders could develop a plan to improve coordination across the state or within a region. While the interviewees from institutions did not have specific suggestions for how the state could improve coordination, one potential model is the Guided Pathways movement, which has brought together cohorts of institutions that engage in common planning. States could also build into the program approval process a requirement that institutions demonstrate that they are not duplicating programs and are addressing a unique need. In Ohio, where a market analysis is required for program approval at the state level, an institution is required to justify its proposed program if a neighboring institution already provides similar offerings; these requirements can help prompt institutions to work more cooperatively. Encouraging institutions to work together on identifying programs to offer would also allow institutions to focus on programs that reflect their unique strengths, resulting in a more-robust and intentional set of options for students. As of 2023, Colorado has three consortia in development: Colorado Online, which offers course and program sharing and shared student and IT services; Rural College Consortium, which focuses on synchronous courses and sharing services for rural institutions; and Colorado Skills Institute, which provides institutions with opportunities to offer courses statewide. While these efforts are crucial to enhancing institutional capacities and expanding opportunities for all students, states should build on this momentum to better align course work, transferability of credits, and stackability of credential options.

In both Colorado and Ohio, state leaders have begun to promote coordination among institutions at a more-systematic level by developing state initiatives to promote the transferability of credits across institutions, and the awarding of credit for noncredit learning. However, according to some interviewees, there continue to be challenges with coordination across institutions and perceptions that credits are articulated unequally between institutions, leading to circumstances that might require students to take additional courses to satisfy credential requirements. States could consider reviewing the criteria for transferability and clarifying the statewide standards for articulation.

Provide Additional Funding for Instructional Resources

A lack of instructional resources can hinder program development, and equipment in fields such as welding and nursing can be expensive. Some interviewees noted that this can be a particular challenge for rural institutions that serve relatively few students and cannot share resources with other institutions. State leaders might consider providing supplemental funding to institutions interested in expanding stackable options, prioritizing under-resourced and rural institutions. In fact, Ohio, through the Regionally Aligned Priorities in Delivering Skills program, has already provided $47 million in funding for institutions to purchase equipment and build training facilities (e.g., laboratories). State and institutional leaders might also consider collaborating with industry partners who could facilitate sharing of equipment across institutions. For example, in Ohio, joint technical training sites were developed so that technical programs serving adult learners and high school students could leverage the same equipment and share costs.

Barrier Three: Insufficient Information and Resources to Identify and Stack Credentials of Value

As described in Chapter 2, individuals need information and resources to understand how to stack credentials and select credentials that will offer value in terms of increased earnings. If individuals lack information about how different programs fit together and how different credentials will help expand job opportunities, they might choose low-return credentials and might not reenroll after obtaining the first credential. We first examine evidence from administrative data on the returns from stacking in different fields and the degree to which low-income individuals are concentrated in low-return fields. We then describe stakeholder perceptions regarding awareness of stackable credential programs, and our review of the information and resources available on institutional websites. Finally, we conclude with stakeholder perspectives on the factors that limit the available information about and resources for stackable programs and the actions that states and institutions can take to expand stackable credential information.

Evidence from Administrative Data on the Sorting of Low-Income Students into Fields with Different Returns

While we cannot directly examine how individuals are using information, the sorting of individuals into low-return and high-return fields might be an indicator of informational issues. If low-income certificate-earners have inadequate access to information on credential value when making decisions about which fields of study to pursue, they might be disproportionately concentrated in low-return fields. To quantitatively assess this possibility, we examined labor market returns from stacking in select fields of study and related this information to our findings on the fields that disproportionately enroll low-income certificate-earners (allied health, education and FCS, mechanics, and nursing in both states; culinary and personal services in Colorado; and design and applied arts in Ohio) versus those that disproportionately enroll middle- and high-income certificate-earners (business, IT, MET, and security and protective services and related fields in both states; design and applied arts in Colorado; and culinary and personal services in Ohio).

Low-income certificate-earners were concentrated in some of the fields least likely to result in a middle-income wage (see Figure 5.6). In Colorado, two of the three fields with the greatest percentage of low-income certificate-earners, education and FCS and culinary and personal services, had by far the lowest percentages of stackers earning a middle-income wage. In Ohio, we see the same pattern for education and FCS and

FIGURE 5.6

Concentration of Low-Income Certificate-Earners and Poststacking Attainment of a Middle-Income Wage for Common Fields of First Certificate, by State

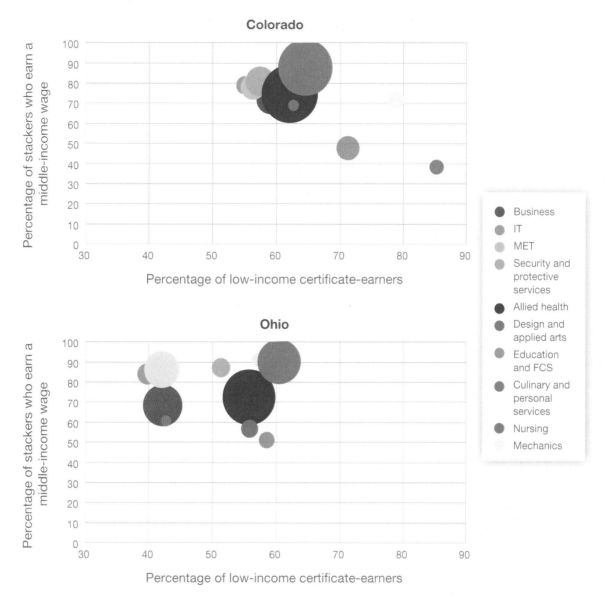

SOURCE: Authors' calculations using data from the CCCS and OLDA.

NOTES: *N* = 32,784 certificate-earners in Colorado, and *N* = 40,485 certificate-earners in Ohio. The sample included students who earned their first certificate in one of the ten listed fields of study from a CCCS college or Ohio community college between July 1, 2006, and June 30, 2015. The measure of the percentage of stackers who earn at least a middle-income wage was further limited to those who earned a stacked credential within three years of their first certificate. *Middle-income wage* was defined as annualized quarterly earnings > 200 percent of the FPL. Wages were adjusted to 2020 first-quarter dollars using the CPI-U. The size of the circle represents the relative number of certificate-earners in that field. The ten fields of study listed here accounted for approximately 90 percent of certificate-earners in Colorado and Ohio, and descriptions of each field are in the appendix.

design and applied arts. Low-income certificate-earners were also underrepresented in several fields with high rates of middle-income wage attainment, including MET and IT, especially in Ohio.

That said, two fields of study, mechanics and nursing, appear promising for low-income certificate-earners. About 70 percent of Colorado's stackers in mechanics and upward of 80 percent of Ohio's stackers in mechanics earned at least a middle-income wage, and, in both states, mechanics had a relatively high concentration of low-income certificate-earners. Nursing was similarly promising as a high-return field with many low-income certificate-earners.

Evidence on Student Awareness and the Information Available on Stackable Programs

We drew on our interviews with stakeholders and a scan of 13 community college websites across the two states to describe the information available to students on stackable credentials and the degree to which students might be aware of stackable credential options.

Institutional staff reported that students are often not aware of stackable credential options, although this awareness can vary depending on a given individual's familiarity with the culture of higher education (i.e., having the skills and knowledge to navigate institutional policies, supports, and services) and the role of industry. In some instances, companies source out their professional development to local community colleges, which might expose employees to opportunities to further their education. Institutional representatives reported that marketing efforts tended to be underfunded and uncoordinated, and outreach efforts did not effectively deliver useful information to individuals about the benefits (e.g., potential opportunities and increase in salaries, program flexibility) of short-term credentials and stackable options.

College websites are one place where many institutions place information on credentials and pathways that could help individuals make decisions and facilitate stacking, and they are likely to be primary resources for incoming and current students. In our review of community college websites in Colorado and Ohio, we found considerable variation in terms of their comprehensiveness and user-friendliness. Some offered comprehensive information that was laid out in an accessible way. For example, one website had a page for each credential that presented a summary of the credential with a link to a more-detailed description, courses and credit hours by semester, Ohio universities where the credential would transfer to a bachelor's degree, and a "related careers" box summarizing careers and median wages. The webpages allowed users to discover more detailed information by expanding boxes on the page so that all information about the credential fit on one page. Other websites had less comprehensive information and were more difficult to navigate. On some websites, the information offered and the format in which it was presented varied across programs, which might impede the ability to explore and compare programs.

We examined websites for evidence of critical information for decisionmaking in six areas and found the following:

- *Course requirements for credentials.* All websites had links from credentials to courses and the number of hours or credits required to earn the credential, and almost all websites presented this information clearly.
- *Learning outcomes for credentials.* Most websites presented learning outcomes for credentials. However, the level of detail varied considerably between websites. Some websites provided a level of detail that would help students make decisions about credentials, but most provided relatively undetailed statements of learning outcomes.
- *Linkage of credentials to industry-recognized certificates.* Most websites referenced industry-recognized credentials related to certificates. The most frequently referenced industry-recognized credentials were for the mechanics, health care, and IT fields. This might be because industry-recognized credentials are more important for advancement in these fields than in others.
- *Mapping of credentials to degrees.* Websites varied on whether they showed how credit from credentials could help students earn a degree. Some websites for Ohio institutions showed how their credentials would transfer to degrees at colleges or universities, but many did not show this information explicitly.

Often, the extent to which websites mapped credentials to degrees varied among programs within an institution.

- *Connection of credentials to careers and earnings.* Most websites presented median earnings for occupations associated with credentials from at least some programs. Some sites offered useful details by presenting earnings for "entry," "average," and "experienced" workers or by allowing users to filter to a specific area of the state. Most websites offered descriptions of careers associated with credentials, although the level of detail varied by program and most websites did not offer detailed career information.

- *Information to help choose a course of study.* Most websites provided links to contact information for advisers. Some had links to career assessments or external sources of information about careers, such as O*NET or Glassdoor. One website offered short podcasts produced by the college featuring different occupations and majors. However, none of the websites appeared to offer a user-friendly decision tool to help students choose a course of study.

In conclusion, all websites offered basic information about credentials, and most offered some information on salaries to give a sense of credential value, but the mapping between credentials and details on how they stack was not always communicated clearly. Few websites provided comprehensive information packaged in a user-friendly design. There might be opportunities for improving the website materials available to individuals to ensure that materials communicate the stackable nature of programs in a straightforward way.

Stakeholder Perspectives on Factors Related to Insufficient Information to Support Selection of Stackable Programs

The findings above suggest that low-income individuals are sorting into some low-return fields, and our discussions with stakeholders and review of website information suggested that there might be issues with awareness of stackable credential programs among those individuals who could potentially benefit from them and limited information to support this awareness. Stakeholders reflected on what might contribute to limited awareness of stackable credential programs and described three main factors.

Common Perceptions on College Credentials and Certain Fields

In our conversations, institutional representatives emphasized the difficulty of communicating options to stack credentials and their associated benefits because of individuals' perspectives on the value, affordability, and flexibility of postsecondary education. According to institutional administrators and system leaders, many individuals in the workforce (and employers) do not see the value of receiving college credit or earning a college degree. Individuals might perceive college as a costly, long-term commitment and might be more interested in getting a job or learning a marketable skill. Individuals might also feel that their technical coursework in high school or at a training center or their industry-recognized credential is sufficient to be hired at a satisfactory wage. This is true in many cases because employers often hire postsecondary students who have gained useful skills but who have not yet earned a college degree. These perceptions can also be amplified by students' cultural perceptions of the types of individuals appropriate for specific fields, leading certain groups to sort into different fields (e.g., women sorting into nursing). Additionally, there might be some fields that are perceived by low-income individuals as challenging to enter or requiring specialized, hard-to-obtain skillsets (e.g., IT).

Interviewees perceived that institutional efforts to counter these views and convey the value of postsecondary credentials were weak and that more could be done to convey the benefits of stackable credentials and expand individuals' perceptions of the different fields available to them. Across our discussions, it seemed that the level of marketing for stackable credentials and associated fields among institutions varied from no effort at all to market to some marketing at the program level.

Limited Messaging from Employers about Credential Value

For many individuals, the information and guidance on which credentials offer value will need to be reinforced by their employers or other trusted voices in industry to make it salient. However, interviewees suggested that individuals receive limited messaging from employers about the value of credentials and, when employers do provide signals about credentials of value, they might not align with the programs offered by institutions. Inconsistent messaging across industry and educational institutions around which credentials offer value can lead to confusion, particularly among historically underserved populations that might have less time to navigate conflicting information.

Constraints on Academic and Faculty Advisors

Students often seek counsel from their instructors and academic advisers to decide on a program of study, but both instructors and advisers face capacity constraints that might limit their ability to support students in choosing credentials of value. Technical centers often have limited funds to hire any advisers, and, at many community colleges, advisers are overstretched and have high rates of turnover. Furthermore, while advisers might have general knowledge about earnings in different fields, they can struggle to provide students in technical fields with detailed career guidance because of unfamiliarity with requirements in specific industries. Instructors at community colleges and technical centers can help fill this gap because they have industry expertise and understand the specific contexts and requirements of an industry, but interviewees from community colleges noted that many instructors (particularly adjunct faculty) do not have the time and capacity to provide this advising support on top of their teaching responsibilities.

Stakeholder Perspectives on Options to Support Informed Student Decisonmaking

There are different ways in which institutions and states might be able to address the factors that contribute to limited information to support student decisionmaking. We describe four of the solutions mentioned most in our stakeholder interviews.

Enhance Informational Resources on Stackable Credentials and Credential Value

Common perceptions about stackable credentials and the value of college programs might be discouraging students from considering further education and training. Our interviewees suggested that institutions could develop additional informational tools and engage in additional outreach efforts to address some of the common perceptions individuals have about postsecondary education that might be discouraging them from pursuing further education and training. The state could also play a role in creating informational resources that support decisionmaking across institutions. For instance, state agencies could create pathways maps (i.e., visuals that convey how credentials fit together and support career advancement) and information toolkits that include general messaging but could be tailored to each institution's context and the workforce opportunities in particular industries and regions. For example, Ohio TechNet created pathways maps for manufacturing to support increased interest in stackable programs in this field, and Ohio Jobs and Family Services is rolling out a new set of online career pathways maps for individuals to learn about opportunities to earn different credentials across fields. Infographics could also be a valuable resource. They are accessible to many individuals and can be broadly disseminated (e.g., through social media) to inform and clarify students' perceptions of the value of stackable credentials.

Provide Institutions with Resources to Enhance Advising Support

Individuals often seek academic advice from their instructors. Faculty, already constrained by their main responsibilities, might not have the time to meet advising needs. Academic advisers could take some pressure off instructors if they had the time and resources to immerse themselves in specific fields and provide more one-on-one support as students navigate transitions through and between programs and into and out of the workforce. Our interviewees suggested that states could provide advisers with virtual training on labor market trends and job requirements so they can help students learn about in-demand occupations and channel their interests into rewarding careers. Academic advisers could also benefit from the information toolkits mentioned previously, which could be shared with students during advising sessions. Although our interviews focused on what postsecondary institutions could do to strengthen stackable credential pipelines, it is likely that advising support needs to be better resourced at the high-school level as well.

Draw on Career Navigation Services

According to the stakeholders we interviewed, institutions could expand the career navigation services they offer alongside academic advising to push back against cultural perceptions that constrain student decisionmaking. Career navigation helps students consider their current circumstances and preferences when choosing fields and jobs. For example, factors that might influence an individual's choice of health care as a career field and their choice of a job within that field include attention to detail, preference for working independently or with other people, aversion to bodily fluid, or prior justice involvement. Moreover, individuals who do not see people like themselves in a specific career field might be discouraged from pursuing stackable pathways that feed into a field that could be a good fit for them. A lack of role models could prevent students from pursuing pathways and credentials of value. Institutions could partner with career centers (and employers) to highlight success stories of employees in nontraditional career fields. For example, one interviewee described a welding program that grew in popularity with women after the career center worked with an employer who brought women welders on campus to talk with students.

Encourage Greater Partnership with Industry

Partnerships between postsecondary institutions and employers can help address some inconsistency in messaging. Our conversations with representatives from postsecondary institutions illuminated three ways that employer partnerships can improve the consistency in messaging that students receive about the value of credentials. First, these partnerships can lead to work-based learning opportunities (e.g., internships, apprenticeships, clinical experiences). These opportunities offer clear messaging to individuals about the value employers place on the programs and credentials that offer these experiences. Second, when employers partner closely with local institutions, the information that both employers and institutions provide to individuals can be more robust and consistent. For example, employers might be better informed about the programs offered by the institution and the value they offer, and institutions might be able to speak more clearly to the added value these credentials will provide in the workplace. In addition, these partnerships might provide more options for institutional representatives to connect with individuals in the workplace and for employer partners to speak on campus about the career opportunities available for individuals with particular credentials. Third, when employers partner with institutions and understand the value of credentials in terms of the skills that employees can develop, they might be more likely to provide the funding and flexibility for employees to pursue these credentials. For example, partnerships could increase the likelihood that employers offer tuition assistance or "earn and learn" arrangements through which incumbent workers spend some designated weekdays on campus to facilitate credential or degree completion without unduly disrupting work. Employers might also be more likely to create clear career incentives (e.g., promotions, increased pay) that link to the completion of a credential.

Yet, as noted in the previous section, institutions face challenges finding the time and resources to cultivate partnerships with employers. The state might need to play a role in helping to provide additional funding to support partnership-building efforts or to coordinate these efforts at a more central level.

Barrier Four: Challenges Moving from Noncredit to Credit Credentials

As described in Chapter 2, the vision for stackable credentials is that they include both noncredit and credit credentials and that individuals can combine for-credit coursework with a wide variety of noncredit credentials, such as industry certifications and licenses and noncredit certificates and badges. There is a broad literature describing the challenges that individuals face when transitioning between noncredit and credit programs and suggesting opportunities for institutions and states to improve opportunities for these transitions. To build on this evidence, we first examine administrative data from Ohio on how noncredit and credit certificate-earners are stacking credentials. We then describe stakeholder perspectives on the factors hindering noncredit-to-credit transitions and actions that states and institutions can take to improve these transitions.

Evidence from Administrative Data on Low-Income Individuals and Noncredit-to-Credit Stacking

As described in Chapter 2, to analyze noncredit-to-credit stacking, we examined a sample of students who either completed a noncredit clock-hour certificate at an OTC or a credit-bearing certificate at an Ohio community college between July 1, 2016, and June 30, 2017. In Figure 5.7, we break down this sample by income status and whether the certificate-earner first completed a noncredit or credit certificate. About 55 percent of noncredit certificate-earners were low-income, compared with 51 percent of credit certificate-earners. The greater prevalence of low-income individuals among noncredit certificate-earners highlights the importance of understanding whether noncredit certificate-earners have opportunities to transition to credit-bearing credential-stacking pathways.

As shown in Table 5.2, low-income certificate-earners who first earned noncredit certificates stacked at higher rates than both middle- and high-income noncredit certificate-earners and low-income individuals

FIGURE 5.7

Certificate-Earners' Income Status in Ohio, by Type of Certificate, 2016–2017

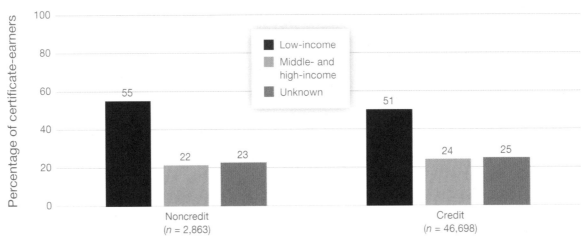

SOURCE: Authors' calculations using data from OLDA.

NOTE: The sample included students who earned their first certificate from an OTC or Ohio community college between July 1, 2016, and June 30, 2017. Noncredit certificates were limited to noncredit clock-hour certificates (or industry credentials). Percentages might not sum to 100 because of rounding.

TABLE 5.2

Noncredit and Credit Certificate-Earners' Stacking Rates in Ohio, by Income, 2016–2017

	First Certificate = Noncredit			First Certificate = Credit		
	Low-Income Certificate-Earners	Middle- and High-Income Certificate-Earners	Difference	Low-Income Certificate-Earners	Middle- and High-Income Certificate-Earners	Difference
Percentage of credentials stacked						
In zero years	50.4%	47.9%	2.5%	20.3%	15.8%	4.5%
In one year	53.8%	49.8%	4.0%	37.8%	31.7%	6.1%
In two years	55.2%	52.1%	3.1%	46.4%	38.9%	7.5%
In three years	56.3%	53.7%	2.6%	49.4%	41.1%	8.3%
N (certificate-earners)	1,587	622		3,385	1,633	

SOURCE: Authors' calculations using data from OLDA.

NOTE: The sample consisted of students who earned their first certificate from an OTC or Ohio community college between July 1, 2016, and June 30, 2017. Noncredit certificates were limited to noncredit clock-hour certificates (or industry credentials). *Stacking* was defined as earning an additional credential of any level, in any field of study, and at any institution within the specified time frame relative to a student's first certificate. We omitted from the table certificate-earners whose income status was unknown.

who first earned credit certificates. Three years after their first certificate, 56 percent of low-income non-credit certificate-earners had stacked, compared with 49 percent of low-income credit certificate-earners.

Although noncredit certificate-earners stacked at higher rates than credit certificate-earners, they often stacked arguably less-valuable credentials. Nearly all low-income and middle- and high-income noncredit certificate-earners (97 percent of each) who stacked credentials earned an additional noncredit certificate, a type of horizontal stacking. Stackers who began with a noncredit certificate also overwhelmingly stacked simultaneously (about 90 percent of both low-income and middle- and high-income stackers); in contrast, about 41 percent of low-income credit certificate-earners and 38 percent of middle- and high-income credit certificate-earners stacked simultaneously (Figure 5.8). This finding suggests that most non-credit certificate-earners who stacked credentials did not obtain work experience in between their initial and stacked credentials. Thus, although noncredit certificate-earners stacked at higher rates than credit certificate-earners, they typically stacked horizontally to a second noncredit certificate and did so at the same time as they earned their first certificate. This pattern was similar for both low-income and middle- and high-income noncredit certificate-earners.

Stakeholder Perspectives on Factors Hindering Noncredit to Credit Transitions

Our findings suggest that low-income individuals in Ohio account for a larger percentage of those who earn noncredit certificates, and very few individuals who earn noncredit certificates ever transition to credit-bearing credentials. Interviewees described four factors that might be contributing to issues with noncredit-to-credit stacking, which have been discussed in the literature as common challenges with noncredit-to-credit transitions across states (e.g., Bahr et al., 2022; Buckwalter and Maag, 2019; Education Strategy Group, 2020; Jacoby, 2019; Jenkins, Lahr, and Mazzariello, 2021; Price and Sedlack, 2018; Rutschow, Tessler, and Lewy, 2021).

FIGURE 5.8

Characteristics of First Certificates and Stacking for Noncredit and Credit Certificate-Earners in Ohio, 2016–2017

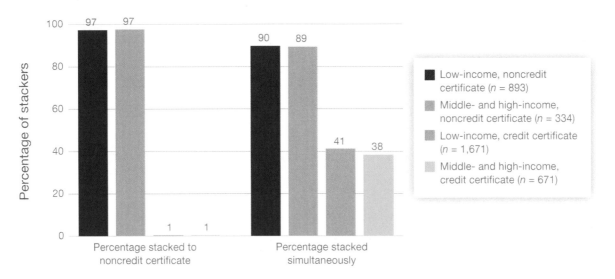

SOURCE: Authors' calculations using data from OLDA.

NOTE: The sample included students who earned their first certificate from an OTC or Ohio community college between July 1, 2016, and June 30, 2017, and earned an additional credential within three years of their first certificate. Noncredit certificates were limited to noncredit clock-hour certificates (or industry credentials). *Simultaneous stacking* was defined as earning a stacked credential on the same date as the first certificate. We omitted from the figure certificate-earners whose income status was unknown.

Administrative Burden

Noncredit-to-credit articulation processes impose burdens of time and monetary cost on staff and students. For example, at some institutions, students are required to take an exam to demonstrate knowledge gained through noncredit learning experiences, but faculty need to develop, update, and administer the exam. In some cases, faculty, advisors, registrars and other staff involved in the enrollment process might need to award credit for noncredit learning experiences on a one-by-one basis, meaning that substantial time might be needed to ensure an individual receives credit for prior learning. Individuals seeking credit for prior non-credit learning also face substantial administrative burden, including requirements to submit documentation and portfolios and pay exam costs, and they might struggle to sufficiently describe or demonstrate skills in a way that meets the institutional requirements for awarding credit.

Lack of Alignment Between Noncredit Learning Experiences and For-Credit Courses

According to administrators at institutions and state and system leaders, the lack of alignment between non-credit learning experiences and specific courses (or perceived lack of alignment) can make awarding credit for noncredit learning difficult. In some cases, noncredit learning experiences might substitute for only the prerequisite to or a portion of a course but not for a full course. In addition, some institutions might award college credit for a noncredit experience that goes on a transcript but does not count toward program require-ments for a credential, which offers limited value to individuals.

Variation in Standards and Perceptions of Quality

Interviews with stakeholders suggested that some have perceptions of noncredit programs as being of lower quality. Noncredit programs are not held to the same accreditation standards, which might be one factor driving these perceptions of lower quality. Noncredit programs at technical centers might also be conflated with credentials from proprietary institutions that offer limited value. These perceptions around value often lead faculty to set rigorous requirements around the demonstration of knowledge and skills from noncredit experiences (e.g., only articulating credit when students can demonstrate knowledge and skills through formal assessments), making it more difficult for noncredit learners to gain faculty approval for noncredit experiences. Some colleges refuse to accept credit from other colleges because they perceive their courses as being better. Accreditation requirements for credit-bearing programs might also limit the ability of institutions to award credit for some noncredit experiences.

Limited Awareness of Articulation Opportunities

Lack of awareness about credit articulation opportunities might keep students from applying to receive credit for their noncredit learning experiences. This lack of awareness exists among students and institutional staff. Incoming students contend with a flood of enrollment information that might drown out information about opportunities to receive credit for noncredit learning. In addition, a student might lack the day-to-day information needed to navigate college, such as information about course checklists or the location of the registrar's office. Relatedly, a lack of awareness among college staff might prevent them from helping students articulate credit for noncredit experiences. Strong partnerships between technical centers and community colleges within a region can support articulation between the institutions, but technical centers lack the ability to educate staff about coursework that could transfer to every college their graduates might attend. Interviewees reported that echnical centers have sometimes received conflicting information from a college and the state and from colleges about the prior learning assessment process.

Stakeholder Perspectives on Options to Improve Noncredit-to-Credit Transitions

Interviewees described four different ways that institutions and system and state leaders can address barriers to moving from noncredit to credit programs.

Streamline Administrative Processes

Administrative burden creates substantial costs related to credit articulation for staff and individuals seeking education and training. To address this issue, state leaders could solicit and disseminate case studies of ways to streamline articulation processes among colleges. Administrators at institutions suggested that state leaders could also advocate for institutions to agree on a standardized approach to marketing noncredit-to-credit opportunities, including clear guidelines that are made available in a prominent place, such as through a link on the college's website. With this approach, students transferring to another institution would know where to seek the information they need to transfer noncredit opportunities to credit-bearing courses. Ohio and Colorado's efforts to establish statewide credit articulation frameworks should help standardize the process by which colleges assess noncredit experience for credit. State efforts might reduce the burden on faculty of translating credit hours and course descriptions across institutions and reduce the burden on students of preparing for exams and seeking out information on institution-specific policies.

Align Noncredit Learning Experiences and For-Credit Courses

To help institutions understand the overlap betwen noncredit learning experiences and for-credit courses and encourage them to articulate credit for noncredit experiences, states could create and update a database that maps industry-recognized credentials to for-credit courses that require similar knowledge or skills content. However, as described above, institutions and individuals might face challenges articulating credit from noncredit learning experiences if those experiences did not cover all the knowledge and skills in a specific for-credit course. To reduce this barrier, colleges and states could map noncredit coursework onto credit-bearing credentials and consider ways to bridge this gap between noncredit learning and the learning outcomes for credit-bearing courses. For example, institutions could further break out courses or credentials to ensure better alignment with common skill sets brought in from noncredit learning experiences. In other words, institutions could offer ways for individuals to cover the additional learning objectives they missed out on through alternative course options and badging or microcredentials. The development of the Colorado Skills Institute, for example, represents a meaningful step for all 13 community colleges in the state to offer noncredit options statewide, thereby creating a space in which future coordination and alignment might occur. Colorado has also developed pathways for students to convert their noncredit training into industry-recognized credentials that could satisfy some requirements for a degree in the fields of IT, cybersecurity, and construction management, suggesting that efforts to better align noncredit training and credit-bearing courses is underway.

Strengthen Coordination Between Credit and Noncredit Departments and Institutions

All of the issues described previously—administrative burden, lack of alignment of noncredit and credit coursework, perceptions of quality, and lack of awareness about articulation options—can be addressed through stronger coordination across noncredit and credit institutions and across noncredit and credit departments within institutions. Interviewees suggested several approaches to coordination that could improve alignment across noncredit and credit programs, including encouraging institutions to adopt standardized transcripts and implementing a common course numbering system in which certain courses have the same numeric identifier and number of credit hours (this system is in place for some parts of coursework in both states, but not for mapping credit and noncredit courses). Such steps could help establish equivalence between learning experiences at different institutions and encourage faculty and staff to articulate credit.

Invest in Outreach to Improve Awareness or Reduce the Need for Awareness

A lack of awareness among individuals seeking education and training and among institutional staff about credit articulation opportunities might prevent individuals from receiving credit for their noncredit learning experiences. Interviewees suggested various approaches that states could take to expand awareness. Colleges and their state agency partners could conduct marketing activities to improve awareness and build databases to identify individuals who might benefit from articulation opportunities and target outreach to those individuals. Institutions could educate advising and enrollment staff on articulation opportunities so that they are better equipped to identify individuals who might be eligible for these opportunities and share them with those individuals. To further encourage faculty to articulate noncredit experience, states and institutions could message the value of noncredit experience and the importance of leveraging this experience for economic development directly to faculty. States could work with institutional leadership to host townhall meetings for faculty to better understand and provide feedback on the efforts to expand articulation of noncredit experiences to credit-bearing programs.

An alternative to outreach strategies that increase awareness is to reduce the need for individuals and staff to seek out information by simplifying processes and articulation frameworks. For example, institutions can build questions about noncredit credentials and learning experiences into enrollment forms and then target information or credit articulation follow-ups to those who are most likely to be eligible, taking the onus of tracking down the information off students. At the state level, the statewide articulation frameworks that both states are pursuing should be helpful in reducing the web of complex, institution-specific articulation policies, and these clear, consistent articulation standards will simplify what individuals and staff need to know about articulation.

CHAPTER 6

Takeaways for States, Systems, and Institutions on Stackable Credentials and Equity

This study pulls together descriptive evidence from two states pursuing stackable credential initiatives to fill two gaps in the literature. We built evidence on whether stackable credentials are helping to advance equity for low-income individuals, and we investigated four systems-level barriers that might contribute to inequities in stackable credential pipelines. Our findings from this work suggest some broader takeaways for the field about stackable credentials and equity.

Continue to scale initiatives that help individuals stack credentials and ensure that these credentials advance equity for historically underserved populations. We find that low-income certificate-earners stacked credentials at rates higher than their middle- and high-income peers and that low-income certificate-earners stacked credentials vertically, which is important because the literature shows that vertical stacking is associated with larger earnings gains (Bohn, Jackson and McConville, 2019; Daugherty and Anderson, 2021). We find that, although income rises for all certificate-earners who stack vertically, the gains are particularly large for low-income certificate-earners, leading to a narrowing of the average income gaps for these groups of students. While stacking helped to reduce gaps between low-income and middle- and high-income individuals, it did not fully eliminate them, suggesting that these credentials alone are insufficient to fully address disparities in income and individuals might require additional education and training or other supports to move into the middle class. In addition, our deeper inquiry into earnings outcomes across fields points to some fields that enroll large proportions of low-income students yet offer particularly low returns (e.g., culinary arts).

It is also important to note that this positive evidence for low-income certificate-earners stands in contrast to findings for other historically underserved groups; studies indicate that individuals of color and older individuals go on to stack credentials at lower rates and see smaller earnings gains relative to White individuals and younger individuals (Bohn and McConville, 2018; Bohn, Jackson and McConville, 2019; Daugherty et al., 2020; Daugherty and Anderson, 2021). Although we suspect many low-income individuals are also individuals of color, the findings suggest that there are inequities within stackable credential pipelines that might be more strongly tied to race, ethnicity, and age than to socioeconomic status. It is also possible that many low-income individuals never complete a first certificate and thus do not enter a stackable credential pathway. The low-income students who successfully complete a first certificate and enter a stackable credentials pathway might be especially well positioned to succeed in that pathway. Future research might consider whether there are income-based inequities to entry to a stackable credentials program. It is important to investigate these other disparities in greater depth to understand what might be driving different patterns in stacking and lower employment returns for students of color and adult learners and to strengthen stackable credential pipelines to address the sources of inequities.

Identify and scale credentials of value. We consider credentials of value to be those that offer improved career opportunities for individuals. In this study, our measures of earnings gains capture one critical measure of value. Fields such as IT, MET, mechanics, and nursing all offer high returns to individuals who stack credentials, and these are the types of programs that states and institutions should be looking to scale. Particularly in nursing, a field with low stacking rates, it will be important for states and institutions to consider how to encourage more stackable program development and support individuals in earning multiple credentials. On the other hand, states and institutions should carefully consider whether to offer programs in fields such as education and FCS, culinary and personal services, and design and applied arts that provide graduates with limited earnings gains despite opportunities to stack credentials.

Invest resources strategically to ensure that stackable credential pipelines are equitable and identify opportunities for additional coordination and alignment. Building stackable credential pipelines requires many different stakeholders and substantial resources. Colorado and Ohio are already making substantial investments in stackable credential programs through formula funding for certificates, scholarships for short-term credentials, and other budget items that support equipment and program design. However, many of the suggestions from stakeholders focused on getting additional resources to cover program startup costs, industry engagement efforts, equipment, faculty, and other inputs that make the development of new programs in some fields and institutions difficult. State agencies and systems could explore where they might provide additional funding to support these costs. Institutional leaders might also need to prioritize the use of internal funds for these programs. In addition, given the broad set of stakeholders and institutions involved in stackable credential pipelines, the need for coordination and alignment was a prominent and commonly noted challenge in our stakeholder interviews. State agencies and college systems can play valuable roles in establishing structures that require coordination and alignment. For example, both Ohio and Colorado are pursuing statewide frameworks that articulate noncredit learning experiences to credit-bearing coursework. Requiring coordination with other institutions in the region prior to program development and facilitating opportunities for institutions to engage with industry are other examples of ways that states and college systems facilitate coordination between institutions.

Ensure that low-income individuals and other historically underserved populations have clear information on stackable programs and credential value. Drawing on the prior literature (e.g., Duke-Benfield et al., 2019; Karp, 2013) and our conversations with stakeholders, the evidence suggests that individuals are not always well informed about their options and the value of different programs and credential pathways. Individuals are not being equipped with the information and resources to understand credential value, and limited information on credential value might be a particular barrier for low-income individuals (and other historically underserved populations) who do not have the time and experience to independently seek out this information (Duke-Benfield et al., 2019; Karp, 2013). To better support individuals in choosing credentials of value, institutions and states can increase funding for career services and advising and improve industry partnerships that could elevate awareness of stackable credentials.

Continue to pursue efforts to support noncredit-to-credit movement, including the collection of better noncredit data. Prior research indicates that opportunities to stack vertically can be valuable for individuals (Bohn, Jackson, and McConville, 2019; Daugherty and Anderson, 2021), and returns from stacking credit-bearing credentials can exceed returns to noncredit credentials (Daugherty and Anderson, 2021; Hester and Kitmitto, 2020). Yet, our study and others (e.g., Bahr et al., 2022; Daugherty et al., 2020; Xu and Ran, 2020) show relatively few individuals transitioning from noncredit to credit programs. Both Ohio and Colorado are leading statewide efforts to build noncredit-to-credit articulation frameworks, so those efforts should support noncredit-to-credit transitions. Stakeholders recommended additional strategies—such as reducing administrative burden, aligning programs, and building awareness—that are echoed in the literature (e.g., Buckwalter and Maag, 2019; Education Strategy Group, 2020; Rutschow, Tessler, and Lewy, 2021).

While this report helps to advance the knowledge around socioeconomic disparities in stacking and the systemic barriers to equity within stackable credential pipelines, more work is needed. Our framework emphasized four systems-level barriers that we were able to explore through administrative data. We excluded critical factors that might act as barriers to equity within stackable credential pipelines, such as how institutional staff engage with students, the academic requirements underlying particular programs, and financial aid availability. And because we grounded our analyses of quantitative evidence in an exploration of socioeconomic disparities, we have little to say about how barriers to equity are playing a role in driving disparities by race, ethnicity, and age.

We also focused explicitly on a sample of individuals who had already earned a certificate, which are a subset of all individuals who might be affected by stackable credentials. Although this was appropriate given the focus of our analysis on attainment of a second credential, our report does not address barriers to completing an initial certificate, which is often the first step in a stackable credentials pipeline.

And our data were limited in a few important ways. Our quantitative data document patterns of stacking, but we cannot directly examine the programs offered and different components shaping access within the system and institutions. We also had incomplete data on noncredit credentials, limiting our ability to fully observe stacking of these credentials. Our qualitative investigation focused on a limited set of perspectives and did not incorporate data on the experiences of the individuals facing barriers within stackable credential programs, and, while we talked to a few administrators, faculty, and staff, we did not broadly capture the perspectives of those responsible for developing stackable programs and supporting student enrollment in and completion of these programs. To gain a deep understanding of equity in stackable credential pipelines, research should incorporate evidence from these key stakeholders.

CHAPTER 7

Conclusion

Stackable credentials have been growing in popularity since the mid-2000s and are an important focus of many state and institutional initiatives to strengthen applied programs in fields such as health care, IT, and advanced manufacturing. These programs aim to open more pathways into and through postsecondary education for historically underserved populations, including low-income individuals. The evidence presented in this report suggests that low-income students are stacking credentials at higher rates than middle- and high-income students, and that when low-income individuals go on to earn degrees, it reduces gaps in earnings. States and institutions should continue to build out stackable programs and ensure that they reach the diverse set of individuals who can benefit from education and training and the variety of workforce needs.

States and institutions have more work to do to ensure that stackable credential pipelines are accessible and structured to promote equitable experiences and outcomes. Our findings contribute to prior literature indicating wide variation in the value of credentials and opportunities to stack those credentials across fields. While low-income individuals were seeing meaningful earnings gains from vertical stacking and from stacking in certain fields of study, horizontal stacking and stacking in other fields (e.g., education and FCS) did not appear to provide meaningful returns to low-income individuals. For these credentials and pathways that do not offer value to low-income individuals, states and institutions must either find ways to strengthen programs and identify opportunities for more-valuable stacking opportunities or eliminate programs and steer students away from them.

While many of the findings were favorable for low-income students and did not suggest socioeconomic disparities of concern, prior research suggest that students of color and adult learners might be stacking less and seeing smaller earnings gains from stacking credentials. Little is understood about what is driving these patterns. The findings from our discussions with stakeholders help unpack some factors that might be driving inequities and possible solutions to addressing the barriers, but additional work is needed to fully understand how stackable credentials are supporting historically underserved populations.

Detailed Description of Data and Methods

Administrative Data Analysis

Data Sources

CCCS and ODHE (via OLDA) provided data for this study. CCCS provided student-level administrative data on demographic characteristics, enrollments, course-taking, credentials earned, and financial aid applications for students enrolled at one of its 13 state community colleges. We did not have administrative data for Colorado's two local district community colleges (Aims Community College and Colorado Mountain College) or its area technical colleges (Emily Griffith Technical College, Pickens Technical College, and Technical College of the Rockies). These data also included matched student-quarter wage records derived from Colorado's UI database.

ODHE provided comparable data for its entire system of public two- and four-year colleges and universities, including its 23 community colleges. The exception was financial aid application data, which were unavailable for Ohio students. The OLDA data also covered enrollments in its public career centers and OTCs.[1] OTCs offer training that culminates in noncredit certificates, but they do not award degrees or credit certificates. The data we obtained from CCCS spanned academic years 2006–2007 through 2019–2020, while ODHE data covered academic years 2001–2002 through 2019–2020.

Both agencies also provided matched records obtained from NSC, which tracks enrollments and graduation across all participating postsecondary institutions. NSC estimated that its records cover approximately 97 percent of students enrolled in U.S. postsecondary institutions (Dundar and Shapiro, 2016). These data enabled us to identify credential-stacking that occurred outside the 13 CCCS institutions and the Ohio public system, resulting in a much more complete picture of credential-stacking.

Sample

Our primary sample was composed of students who completed their first-ever observed undergraduate credit certificate (short or long) at one of the 13 CCCS colleges or one of the 23 Ohio community colleges. We focused on certificate-earners and excluded those whose first observed credential was an associate's degree for several reasons. Certificate-earners typically have lower earnings than those who complete an associate's or bachelor's degree, especially in the long term (Bohn, Jackson, and McConville, 2019; Giani and Fox, 2017). Moreover, prior research on credential-stacking has likewise found that students whose first credential was a certificate were most likely to benefit from stacking (e.g., Daugherty and Anderson, 2021).

We further restricted our sample to students age 20 to 64 who were residents of Colorado or Ohio in the term of their first certificate. These restrictions increased the probability that our sample consisted of certificate-earners who have the UI records necessary to determine their income status: Younger students

---

[1] We excluded records from one OTC, the Ohio Central School System, which provides postsecondary education to incarcerated individuals.

might be less likely to have a sufficient earnings history, and nonresidents might be less likely to be employed in jobs covered by a state's UI system. We also excluded dual-enrollment students or individuals who earned their first observed certificate at institutions other than a CCCS college or Ohio community college. Students might have previously completed an associate's degree or higher at any institution covered by the state administrative or NSC records. In Ohio, the primary sample did not include OTC records, a decision discussed in more detail below. Finally, we excluded a very small number of records missing information on either the date or level of credential (a problem almost exclusive to NSC records), as well as Ohio students without a valid workforce ID.

For our main analysis, we focused on students who earned their first certificate according to the previously described parameters between July 1, 2006, and June 30, 2015. July 1, 2006, marked the beginning of the first academic year for which we had complete administrative data from both Colorado and Ohio. Limiting the analysis to students who completed their first certificate by June 30, 2015, ensured a sufficient follow-up period (up to four years) in which to measure stacking within the constraints of our data. The final samples consisted of 35,663 certificate-earners in Colorado and 45,584 in Ohio.

To facilitate analysis of longer-term returns from stacking, the sample for labor market outcomes analysis was further restricted to students who completed their first certificate between July 1, 2006, and June 30, 2012. This allowed for 24 quarters, or six years, of postcertificate labor market outcomes analysis. This analysis consisted of 23,510 Colorado and 26,277 Ohio certificate-earners. Table A.1 presents summary statistics on the background characteristics of low-income and middle- and high-income certificate-earners in this sample.

TABLE A.1

Demographic Characteristics of Certificate-Earners, by State and Income, Labor Market Analysis Sample, 2006–2012

	Colorado		Ohio	
	Low Income Certificate-Earners	Middle- and High Income Certificate-Earners	Low Income Certificate-Earners	Middle- and High-Income Certificate-Earners
Age				
20–24	39.8%	9.7%	40.3%	4.3%
25–29	21.9%	19.7%	21.6%	17.4%
30–39	20.7%	35.0%	20.6%	33.2%
40–49	11.4%	21.3%	11.9%	27.4%
50–64	6.2%	14.2%	5.7%	17.8%
Mean	30.0	36.7	29.9	39.0
Race/ethnicity				
Asian	2.3%	2.2%	1.4%	0.9%
Black or African American	3.8%	3.7%	11.4%	13.2%
Hispanic	18.6%	12.7%	1.7%	1.8%
White	67.5%	73.4%	81.1%	80.0%
Other	2.8%	2.5%	1.2%	0.9%
Unknown	5.1%	5.4%	3.2%	3.2%

Table A.1—Continued

	Colorado		Ohio	
	Low Income Certificate-Earners	Middle- and High Income Certificate-Earners	Low Income Certificate-Earners	Middle- and High-Income Certificate-Earners
Gender				
Women	64.7%	53.0%	32.6%	45.0%
Men	35.3%	47.0%	67.4%	55.0%
Highest prior degree earned				
Bachelor's degree or higher	13.0%	22.2%	0.9%	1.5%
Associate's degree	3.2%	3.6%	5.8%	5.4%
No prior degree	83.8%	74.2%	93.3%	93.0%
N (certificate-earners)	14,569	5,397	13,557	7,222

SOURCE: Authors' calculations using data from the CCCS and OLDA.

NOTE: The sample consisted of students who earned their first certificate from a CCCS or Ohio community college between July 1, 2006, and June 30, 2012. We omitted from the table certificate-earners whose income status was unknown. Percentages might not sum to 100 because of rounding.

To analyze stacking among students who earned noncredit certificates, we constructed a separate dataset composed of both noncredit certificates (or industry credentials) earned at OTCs and credit certificates and degrees earned at community colleges. The sample consisted of students who first completed either a non-credit certificate at an OTC or a credit certificate at an Ohio community college between July 1, 2016, and June 30, 2017. These additional restrictions were necessary because Ohio's procedures for assigning student identifiers to OTC students differed before and after 2016, rendering earlier data unreliable. The resulting sample consisted of 9,561 noncredit and credit certificate-earners. See Table A.2 for background characteristics for this sample. We did not have data on noncredit credentials in Colorado.

TABLE A.2

Demographic Characteristics of Certificate-Earners in Ohio, by Type of First Certificate and Income, Noncredit Analysis Sample, 2016–2017

	First Certificate = Noncredit		First Certificate = Credit	
	Low Income Certificate-Earners	Middle- and High-Income Certificate-Earners	Low Income Certificate-Earners	Middle- and High-Income Certificate-Earners
Age				
20–24	47.1%	13.2%	45.4%	6.4%
25–29	23.8%	24.1%	24.1%	18.7%
30–39	18.0%	30.5%	17.7%	37.1%
40–49	7.2%	21.2%	8.2%	24.0%
50–64	3.9%	13.5%	4.5%	13.8%
Mean	28.0	35.9	28.5	37.5

Table A.2—Continued

	First Certificate = Noncredit		First Certificate = Credit	
	Low Income Certificate-Earners	Middle- and High-Income Certificate-Earners	Low Income Certificate-Earners	Middle- and High-Income Certificate-Earners
Race/ethnicity				
Asian	0.4%	0.3%	1.4%	1.3%
Black or African American	15.6%	9.0%	14.0%	13.1%
Hispanic	1.2%	1.4%	2.4%	1.8%
White	72.3%	78.0%	74.9%	77.5%
Other	3.1%	1.1%	3.6%	2.0%
Unknown	7.4%	10.1%	3.8%	4.2%
Gender				
Woman	35.5%	68.0%	41.5%	57.0%
Man	64.5%	32.0%	58.5%	43.0%
Highest prior degree earned				
Bachelor's degree or higher	1.2%	3.5%	1.8%	4.2%
Associate's degree	3.8%	5.3%	6.6%	9.6%
No prior degree	95.0%	91.2%	91.6%	86.2%
N (certificate-earners)	1,587	622	3,385	1,633

SOURCE: Authors' calculations using data from OLDA.

NOTE: The sample consisted of students who earned their first certificate from an OTC or Ohio community college between July 1, 2016 ,and June 30, 2017. We omitted from the table certificate-earners whose income status was unknown. Percentages might not sum to 100 because of rounding.

Determining Income Status

We largely drew on student-quarter earnings records derived from Colorado's and Ohio's UI databases to categorize a certificate-earner as low-income or middle- and high-income. Doing so enabled us to avoid issues associated with using students' Pell Grant eligibility or receipt as a determinant of their income, which is perhaps the most-common approach in higher education research. Pell Grant eligibility can only be determined for students who opt to complete the Free Application for Federal Student Aid, and research has demonstrated that many low-income students who are likely to qualify for a Pell Grant never complete the application (Rosinger and Ford, 2019). Moreover, financial aid application data were not available for Ohio certificate-earners, leaving UI data as the only option.

That said, there are some limitations to relying on UI records to determine income status. UI records might underestimate some individuals' earnings because UI records do not cover earnings from self-employment, out-of-state work, or jobs with certain employers, such as the federal government. It is also difficult to use UI records to determine income status for younger students who might not have an established earnings history. Although we minimized the influence of this limitation by restricting the sample to certificate-earners age 20–64, younger individuals are overrepresented in our low-income sample and older individuals are overrepresented in our middle- and high-income sample. This could be an artifact of the availability of UI data for younger students.

To limit the effect of missing UI records in Colorado, we supplemented UI records with financial aid application data. If a certificate-earner had no earnings records for the appropriate time frame but had completed a financial aid application, we used their EFC as a measure of their income. Comparable data were not available for Ohio.

Ideally, we would have used certificate-earners' precollege earnings records to determine their income status. However, our sample was based on cohorts of certificate-earners or completers, not cohorts of entrants, and it was not possible to reliably identify a certificate-earner's entry term or quarter. For example, an individual might have earned their certificate in the second quarter of 2015, after having enrolled in terms corresponding to the second quarter of 2011, the third quarter of 2013, the third quarter of 2014, and the second quarter of 2015. In such a case, it is unclear whether it would be appropriate to treat quarters prior to the second quarter of 2011 or quarters prior to the third quarter of 2013 as that individual's pre-entry quarters.

Given this limitation, we used wage records three years prior to the date of first certificate as a proxy for precollege earnings. More specifically, if the quarter of first certificate is quarter 0, we used a certificate-earner's earnings records from pre-enrollment quarters –9, –10, –11, and –12. Because nearly all certificates require less than two years of full-time coursework to complete (and most require far less), we allowed for up to two potential years of full-time enrollment, during which a student would likely have reduced their workload and wages. Students attending part-time are less likely to reduce their workload or their wages to attend college; thus, this approach also accounts for a part-time enrollment pattern. We used the sum of four quarters to capture a full year of wages in a manner that accounted for any variation due to seasonal employment and to facilitate comparison with thresholds determined on an annual basis.

For certificate-earners with wage records, we defined a *low-income* certificate-earner as a certificate-earner with earnings below 200 percent of the FPL, a threshold commonly used to distinguish between low-income and middle- and high-income individuals (e.g., Bohn, Jackson, and McConville, 2019; Daugherty and Anderson, 2021; Heflin, 2016; Maag et al., 2017). Those with wages at or above 200 percent of the FPL were defined as *middle- and high-income* certificate-earners. For Colorado certificate-earners without wage records but with financial aid application data, we compared their EFCs with the maximum EFC with which a certificate-earner would still be eligible for a Pell Grant. If a certificate-earner's EFC was at or below the threshold for Pell Grant eligibility, we considered that certificate-earner to be low-income; otherwise, that certificate-earner was considered to be middle- and high-income. Income for certificate-earners without wage records in Ohio or without wage and financial aid application records in Colorado was classified as unknown.

We conducted robustness checks using several alternative approaches to determine students' precollege earnings. This included using annualized wages from the quarter nearest to the quarter of first certificate in which a student was not enrolled in college but had wages of at least $100. A second approach involved using the four quarters nearest to the quarter of first certificate, conditional on the student not being enrolled in college in that quarter but having wages of at least $100. Unlike the main approach, these two approaches ensured that the wages measured were not depressed due to college enrollment. For Colorado, we also constructed a sample using only financial aid application data on Pell Grant eligibility to determine income status. Results from these alternatives were comparable to the findings reported using our main approach.

Other Key Measures
We relied on a variety of other measures for analyses.

Types of certificates. This study largely focused on two types of credit certificates, short and long. A short-credit certificate required less than the equivalent of one year of full-time undergraduate credit-bearing coursework to complete, whereas a long-credit certificate required one or more years of such coursework. Some analyses also included noncredit certificates, which required coursework that did not result in academic credits. We limited our analysis to noncredit certificates that qualified as industry credentials.

Stacking. We defined *stacking* as earning a second undergraduate credential within a certain time frame relative to earning a first certificate and included second credentials earned on the same date as the first certificate. Undergraduate credentials included short-credit certificates, long-credit certificates, associate's degrees, and bachelor's degrees. Analysis of noncredit-to-credit credential-stacking also included noncredit certificates. Time frames varied from zero years to four years, but most analyses presented in this report used a three-year time frame. Although the percentage of certificate-earners who stacked increased with longer time frames, general conclusions were similar across time-frame specifications.

Further analysis (not shown here) found that many noncredit certificate-earners completed several noncredit certificates on the same date as their first noncredit certificate. This raised the question of whether focusing on the first stacked credential might have masked subsequent stacking to credit-bearing credentials or staggered stacking among this group of certificate-earners. To examine this possibility, we conducted two additional analyses. First, we redefined *stacked credential* as the highest-level credential earned within three years of a first certificate. Second, we treated all noncredit certificates earned on the same date as the first certificate as a package constituting the first certificate and defined the first credential earned after that date as the stacked credential. Results from these analyses revealed very little additional stacking to credit-bearing credentials and limited staggered stacking, corroborating our main findings.

Characteristics of stacking. For certificate-earners who stacked credentials, we examined three characteristics of the stacked credential. In all cases, we focused on the first observed stacked credential. First, we analyzed the stacked credential as either vertical or horizontal:

- We defined *vertical stacking* as occurring when a certificate-earner completed a second credential that was of a higher level than the first certificate. Specifically, vertical stacking included stacking from a short-credit certificate to a long-credit certificate, associate's degree, or bachelor's degree, or from a long-credit certificate to an associate's or bachelor's degree. When analyzing noncredit-to-credit credential-stacking, vertical stacking included stacking from a noncredit certificate to a short-credit certificate, long-credit certificate, associate's degree, or bachelor's degree.
- We defined *horizontal stacking* as earning a second certificate of the same level or of a lower level than the first certificate. Stacking from a short-credit certificate to a short-credit certificate, from a long-credit certificate to a long-credit certificate, or from a long-credit certificate to a short-credit certificate were all types of horizontal stacking. For analysis that included noncredit certificates, stacking from a noncredit certificate to a noncredit certificate, from a short-credit certificate to a noncredit certificate, or from a long-credit certificate to a noncredit certificate were also considered horizontal.
- For a small percentage of stacked credentials, identified primarily through NSC records, we were able to identify the stacked credential as an undergraduate certificate but unable to categorize the length of the certificate as short or long. Although we defined this as stacking, we did not categorize it as either vertical or horizontal stacking.

We also classified each instance of stacking as either staggered or simultaneous:

- *Staggered* stacking occurred when a stacker earned their stacked credential on any date after the date of their first certificate.
- *Simultaneous* stacking occurred when a stacker earned their stacked credential on the same date as the date of their first certificate.

Finally, we determined whether a stacker earned their second credential in a field related to the field of their first certificate. The definitions below are from Meyer, Bird, and Castleman's (2020) study of credential-stacking, in which they found greater earnings gains for stackers who stacked in the same specific field of study as their first certificate:

- *Stacked in the same specific field.* This is defined as earning a second credential classified under the same four-digit CIP code as the first certificate. For example, a stacker might have first earned a short-credit certificate in 47.06 Vehicle Maintenance and Repair Technologies and then earned a long-credit certificate with the same CIP code.
- *Stacked in the same broad field, but in a different specific field.* Stackers in this category earned their second credential in a different four-digit CIP code than their first certificate, but within the same broad field or two-digit CIP code. For instance, a stacker earning a long-credit certificate in 52.04 Business Operations Support and Assistant Services followed by an associate's degree in 52.02 Business Administration, Management, and Operations stacked in the same broad field (business), but in a different specific field.
- *Stacked in a different broad field.* This category consists of those stackers who earned their first certificate in one two-digit CIP code, such as 52 Business, Management, Marketing, and Related Support Services and their second credential in a different two-digit CIP code, perhaps 11 Computer and Information Sciences and Support Services.

Labor market outcomes. We measured earnings as an individual's annualized quarterly earnings, conditional on employment (i.e., on having a record of wages > $100) in that quarter. We also top-coded all wages greater than the 99th percentile (based on all wage records from the observation window). All earnings were converted to 2020 first-quarter dollars using the CPI-U. We considered an individual to earn at least a middle-income wage if their annualized earnings in a quarter exceed 200 percent of the FPL for that calendar year. This measure was conditional on employment as defined previously.

Field of study. Although we conducted analyses involving field of study at the four-digit and two-digit CIP code levels, we aggregated most of our findings into 11 categories. Table A.3 describes the two-digit and, where applicable, four-digit CIP codes that apply to each of these 11 fields of study. Note that only two-digit CIP codes were available for noncredit-to-credit transition analysis.

Qualitative Methods

The purpose of conducting qualitative research was to improve our understanding of the barriers to building and expanding stackable credential programs. Our qualitative research design was guided by our conceptual framework, quantitative data across both states, and discussions with members of our technical advisory boards. First, to understand how the four systems-level barriers operated in Colorado and Ohio, we analyzed state data to identify institutions that represented a variety of different settings serving low-income student populations. We first limited our interview sample to institutions serving large populations of Pell Grant–eligible students. We then chose institutions according to rates of stacking for those earning certificates in health care, IT, and MET to ensure that we were capturing institutions with low, high, and mixed stacking rates. We also chose institutions that reflected different regions (urban, suburban, and rural), sizes, and institutional mission (community colleges, technical centers, and four-year universities). In focusing on this sample of institutions, we hoped to capture a representative set of institutions serving low-income communities. We then shared the targeted sample with our technical advisory boards, which offered institutional-level context to inform our final list of institutions. Lastly, systems- and state-level perspectives were included to

TABLE A.3

Descriptions of Fields of Study

Field of Study	Description
Allied health	All programs classified under CIP 51 Health Professions and Related Clinical Studies excluding CIP codes 51.38 and 51.39
Business	All programs classified under CIP 52 Business, Management, Marketing, and Related Support Services
Culinary and personal services	All programs classified under CIP 12 Personal and Culinary Services
Design and applied arts	All programs classified under CIP 50 Visual and Performing Arts, with a majority classified under 50.04 Design and Applied Arts
Education and FCS	All programs classified under CIP 13 Education or CIP 19 Family and Consumer Sciences/Human Sciences
IT	All programs classified under CIP 11 Computer and Information Sciences and Support Services
MET	All programs classified under CIP 14 Engineering, CIP 15 Engineering Technologies/Technicians, or CIP 48 Precision Production
Mechanics	All programs classified under CIP 47 Mechanic and Repair Technologies/Technicians, with the vast majority classified as 47.06 Vehicle Maintenance and Repair Technologies
Nursing	Programs classified under CIP 51.38 Registered Nursing, Nursing Administration, Nursing Research, and Clinical Nursing or CIP 51.39 Practical Nursing, Vocational Nursing, and Nursing Assistants
Security and protective services	All programs classified under CIP 43 Security and Protective Services
All others	All programs classified under two-digit CIP codes not listed above

SOURCE: National Center for Education Statistics, undated.

better understand the significance of the barriers that institutions encounter. On the recommendation of our technical advisory boards, key systems- and state-level postsecondary leaders were identified and included in our list for recruitment.

Across both states, we invited 36 organizations to participate in the study. Each organization received up to three email invitations. If we did not receive a response after two weeks of sending the third email invitation, we ceased recruitment efforts with those organizations. We involved our technical advisory board members by making introductions to their contacts at institutions that were not immediately responsive to our invitation. Our efforts led to a total of 20 organizations participating in the study (see Table A.4 for a complete list). In Colorado, this included three technical centers, five community colleges, one four-year university, CCCS, and one state-level higher education agency. In Ohio, the organizations included two OTCs, three community colleges, two four-year universities, and two state-level higher education agencies. Our contacts at each site consisted of academic administrators and faculty across the different institution types, senior administrators at systems-level organizations, and educational policy leaders at the state-level agencies. Semistructured interviews were conducted when an individual's schedule was not aligned with their colleagues participating in the focus group or if an organization or agency had only one individual to speak on issues related to stackable credentials; this occurred once for a four-year university in Colorado and for a state-level agency in Ohio. Outside those cases, focus groups were conducted.

TABLE A.4

List of Participating Organizations, by State and Type

Organization	Colorado	Ohio
Community college	Arapahoe Community College Northeastern Junior College Pueblo Community College	Lorain County Community College Stark State College Zane State College
Technical center	Emily Griffith Technical College Pickens Technical College Technical College of the Rockies	Career and Technology Education Centers of Licking County Penta Career Center
Four-year university	Colorado State University System Metropolitan State University-Denver	University of Cincinnati Ohio University
State-level agency	CCCS Colorado Department of Higher Education	ODHE OTCs

Data collection was conducted virtually through ZoomGov. Semistructured interviews were 60 minutes long, whereas focus groups lasted no more than 90 minutes. To ensure validity, protocol question topics and questions were organized by and sensitive to the four barriers in the conceptual framework. Some protocol questions were modified to better align with the roles and responsibilities of our participants. Notes were taken during the interviews and focus groups to ensure that individuals felt secure to participate in the study. Analysis of the data was conducted through Dedoose, a qualitative analytic software. We drew on the conceptual framework and prior literature to develop a codebook, which was organized by the four barriers. While the codebook was a helpful guide to our analysis, we also coded for new topics and concepts that emerged organically from the data. Two researchers coded the data, focusing on key constructs and the relationships between constructs to organize the themes that emerged from our research questions. Through this process, researchers identified and reconciled discrepancies between their analyses.

Abbreviations

CCCS	Colorado Community College System
CIP	Classification of Instructional Programs
CPI-U	Consumer Price Index for All Urban Consumers
EFC	Expected Family Contribution
FCS	family and consumer sciences
FPL	Federal Poverty Level
IT	information technology
MET	manufacturing and engineering technology
NSC	National Student Clearinghouse
ODHE	Ohio Department of Higher Education
OLDA	Ohio Longitudinal Data Archive
OTC	Ohio Technical Center
TAACCCT	Trade Adjustment Assistance Community College and Career Training
UI	unemployment insurance

References

Anderson, Drew M., and Lindsay Daugherty, "Community Colleges Can Increase Credential Stacking by Introducing New Programs Within Established Technical Pathways," *Journal of Higher Education*, February 10, 2023.

Austin, James T., Gail O Mellow, Mitch Rosin, and Marlene Seltzer, *Portable, Stackable Credentials: A New Education Model for Industry-Specific Career Pathways*, McGraw-Hill Research Foundation, November 28, 2012.

Bahr, Peter Riley, *The Earnings of Community College Graduates in California*, Center for Analysis of Postsecondary Education and Employment, December 2016.

Bahr, Peter Riley, Rooney Columbus, Kennan Cepa, Jennifer May-Trifiletti, and Samuel Kaser, *Investigating the Hidden College: A Study of Community College Noncredit Education in Five States*, University of Michigan and Opportunity America, December 2022.

Bahr, Peter Riley, Susan Dynarski, Brian Jacob, Daniel Kreisman, Alfredo Sosa, and Mark Wiederspan, "Labor Market Returns to Community College Awards: Evidence from Michigan," working paper, Center for Analysis of Postsecondary Education and Employment, March 2015.

Bailey, Thomas, and Clive R. Belfield, "Stackable Credentials: Awards for the Future?" working paper, Community College Research Center, Columbia University, April 2017a.

Bailey, Thomas, and Clive R. Belfield, "Stackable Credentials: Do They Have Labor Market Value?" working paper, Community College Research Center, Columbia University, November 2017b.

Belfield, Clive, and Thomas Bailey, "The Labor Market Returns to Sub-Baccalaureate College: A Review," working paper, Center for Analysis of Postsecondary Education and Employment, March 2017.

Bennett, Mary P., Sherry Lovan, Marian Smith, and Chandra Elllis-Griffith, "Nursing's Leaky Pipeline: Barriers to a Diverse Nursing Workforce," *Journal of Professional Nursing*, Vol. 37, No. 2, March–April 2021.

Bettinger, Eric, and Adela Soliz, "Returns to Vocational Credentials: Evidence from Ohio's Community and Technical Colleges," working paper, Center for Analysis of Postsecondary Education and Employment, October 2016.

Blume, Grant, Elizabeth Meza, Debra Bragg, and Ivy Love, *Estimating the Impact of Nation's Largest Single Investment in Community Colleges: Lessons and Limitations of a Meta-Analysis of TAACCCT Evaluations*, New America Foundation, October 7, 2019.

Bohn, Sarah, Jacob Jackson, and Shannon McConville, *Career Pathways and Economic Mobility at California's Community Colleges*, Public Policy Institute of California, June 2019.

Bohn, Sarah, and Shannon McConville, *Stackable Credentials in Career Education at California Community Colleges*, Public Policy Institute of California, October 2018.

Buckwalter, Veronica, and Taylor Maag, *Closing the Credit-Noncredit Divide: Bridging the Gap in Postsecondary Education to Expand Opportunity for Low-Wage Working Adults*, Jobs for the Future, October 2019.

Center for Occupational Research and Development, *Stackable Credentials Tool Kit*, U.S. Department of Education, April 2018.

Center for Occupational Research and Development, *Introduction to Stackable Credentials,* Office of Career, Technical, and Adult Education, U.S. Department of Education, January 2021.

Cleary, Jennifer, and Michelle Van Noy, "A Framework for Higher Education Labor Market Alignment: Lessons and Future Directions in the Development of Jobs-Driven Strategies," working paper, Heldrich Center for Workforce Development, Rutgers University, October 2014.

Colorado Department of Higher Education, "Enrollment," dashboard, undated. As of March 7, 2023: https://cdhe.colorado.gov/data-and-research/tools/dashboard/enrollment

Colorado General Assembly, Opportunities for Credential Attainment, State Bill 22-192, May 26, 2022.

Credential Engine, *Counting U.S. Postsecondary and Secondary Credentials*, 2022.

Daugherty, Lindsay, and Drew M. Anderson, *Stackable Credential Pipelines in Ohio: Evidence on Programs and Earnings Outcomes*, RAND Corporation, RR-A207-1, 2021. As of February 23, 2023: https://www.rand.org/pubs/research_reports/RRA207-1.html

Daugherty, Lindsay, Jenna W. Kramer, Drew M. Anderson, Robert Bozick, *Stacking Educational Credentials in Ohio: Pathways Through Postsecondary Education in Health Care, Manufacturing and Engineering Technology, and Information Technology*, RAND Corporation, RR-A136-1, 2020. As of February 23, 2023: https://www.rand.org/pubs/research_reports/RRA136-1.html

de Brey, Cristobal, Lauren Musu, Joel McFarland, SydneyWilkinson-Flicker, Melissa Diliberti, Anlan Zhang, Claire Branstetter, and Xiaolei Wang, *Status and Trends in the Education of Racial and Ethnic Groups 2018*, National Center for Education Statistics, U.S. Department of Education, February 2019.

Duke-Benefield, Amy Ellen, Bryan Wilson, Kermit Kaleba, and Jenna Leventoff, *Expanding Opportunities: Defining Quality Non-Degree Credentials for States*, National Skills Coalition, September 2019.

Dundar, Afet, and Doug Shapiro, *The National Student Clearinghouse as an Integral Part of the National Postsecondary Data Infrastructure*, National Student Clearinghouse Research Center, May 2016.

Education Strategy Group, *A More Unified Community College: Strategies and Resources to Align Non-Credit and Credit Programs*, October 6, 2020.

Employment and Training Administration, "Increasing Credential, Degree, and Certificate Attainment by Participants of the Public Workforce System," Training and Employment Guidance Letter No. 15-10, U.S. Department of Labor, December 15, 2010.

Ganzglass, Evelyn, *Scaling "Stackable Credentials": Implications for Implementation and Policy*, Center for Postsecondary and Economic Success, March 2014.

Giani, Matthew, and Heather Lee Fox, "Do Stackable Credentials Reinforce Stratification or Promote Upward Mobility? An Analysis of Health Professions Pathways Reform in a Community College Consortium," *Journal of Vocational Education & Training*, Vol. 69, No. 1, 2017.

Heflin, Colleen, "Family Instability and Material Hardship: Results from the 2008 Survey of Income and Program Participation," *Journal of Family & Economic Issues*, Vol. 37, No. 3, September 2016.

Hester, Candace, and Sami Kitmitto, *The Relative Returns to Credit- and Non-Credit-Bearing Credentials*, American Institutes for Research, October 2020.

Holzer, Harry, *Job Market Polarization and U.S. Worker Skills: A Tale of Two Middles*, Brookings Institution, April 2015.

Hoxby, Caroline M., and Sarah Turner, "What High-Achieving Low-Income Students Know About College," *American Economic Review*, Vol. 105, No. 5, May 2015.

Jacoby, Tamar, *Community College Career Education: Scaling a New Approach*, Lumina Foundation, July 2019.

Jenkins, Davis, Hana Lahr, and Amy Mazzariello, *How to Achieve More Equitable Community College Student Outcomes*, Community College Research Center, Columbia University, September 2021.

Karp, Melinda, "Entering a Program: Helping Students Make Academic and Career Decisions," working paper, Community College Research Center, Columbia University, May 2013.

Kennedy, Brian, Richard Fry, and Cary Funk, "6 Facts About the STEM Workforce," Pew Research Center, April 14, 2021.

Klasik, Daniel, Kristin Blagg, and Zachary Pekor, "Out of the Education Desert: How Limited Local College Options Are Associated with Inequity in Postsecondary Opportunities," *Social Sciences*, Vol. 7, No. 9, September 15, 2018.

Klein-Collins, Rebecca, "Strategies to Produce New Nurses for a Changing Profession: A Policy Brief on Innovation in Nursing Education," Council for Adult and Experiential Learning, 2011.

Maag, Elaine, H. Elizabeth Peters, Anthony Hannagan, Cary Lou, and Julie Siwicki, *Income Volatility: New Research Results with Implications for Income Tax Filing and Liabilities*, Urban Institute and Brookings Institution, May 25, 2017.

Mattern, Krista, and Jeffrey Wyatt, "Student Choice of College: How Far Do Students Go for an Education?" *Journal of College Admission*, Spring 2009.

Meyer, Katharine E., Kelli A. Bird, and Benjamin L. Castleman, "Stacking the Deck for Employment Success: Labor Market Returns to Stackable Credentials," working paper, Annenberg Institute, Brown University, January 2022.

Minaya, Veronica, and Judith Scott-Clayton, "Labor Market Trajectories for Community College Graduates: New Evidence Spanning the Great Recession," *Education Finance and Policy*, Vol. 17, No. 1, Winter 2022.

National Center for Education Statistics, "Browse CIP Codes," webpage, U.S. Department of Education, undated. As of March 1, 2023:
https://nces.ed.gov/Ipeds/cipcode/browse.aspx?y=55

National Center for Education Statistics, "Table 322.20. Bachelor's Degrees Conferred by Postsecondary Institutions, by Race/Ethnicity and Sex of Student: Selected Years, 1976–77 Through 2019–20," U.S. Department of Education, 2021a. As of December 18, 2022:
https://nces.ed.gov/programs/digest/d21/tables/dt21_322.20.asp?current=yes

National Center for Education Statistics, "Table 320.20. Certificates Below the Associate's Degree Level Conferred by Postsecondary Institutions, by Race/Ethnicity and Sex of Student: 1998–99 Through 2019–20," U.S. Department of Education, 2021b. As of December 18, 2022:
https://nces.ed.gov/programs/digest/d21/tables/dt21_320.20.asp?current=yes

Price, Derek V., and Wendy Sedlak, *Creating Opportunity for All: Building Pathways from Continuing Education to Credit Programs*, Achieving the Dream, January 2018.

Rosen, Rachel, and Frieda Molina, *Practitioner Perspectives on Equity in Career and Technical Education*, MDRC, July 2019.

Rosinger, Kelly Ochs, and Karly S. Ford, "Pell Grant Versus Income Data in Postsecondary Research," *Educational Researcher*, Vol. 48, No. 5, June–July 2019.

Rutschow, Elizabeth Zachary, Betsy L. Tessler, and Erika B. Lewy, *Advising for Opportunity: Perspectives and Considerations for Supporting Movement Across Workforce and Academic Programs in Community Colleges*, MDRC, February 2021.

Schmidt, Bonnie, and Brent MacWilliams, "Admission Criteria for Undergraduate Nursing Programs: A Systematic Review," *Nurse Educator*, Vol. 36, No. 4, July–August 2011.

Van Noy, Michelle, Madeline Trimble, Davis Jenkins, Elisabeth Barnett, and John Wachen, "Guided Pathways to Careers: Four Dimensions of Structure in Community College Career-Technical Programs," *Community College Review*, Vol. 44, No. 4, October 2016.

Wilson, Bryan, *Stackable Credential Policy: 50-State Scan*, National Skills Coalition, December 2016.

Xu, Di, and Florence Xiaotao Ran, "Noncredit Education in Community College: Students, Course Enrollments, and Academic Outcomes," *Community College Review*, Vol. 48, No. 1, January 2020.